T0171347

I've had the privilege of knowing Sharon Gresham as a teacher/speaker for many years and now as a writer. Her commitment to in-depth study and application of the Bible is refreshing. The Philippians study equips the pastor/teacher with a resource much needed in the church today. I am excited to teach this study both in our church and as we minister internationally.—*Darrel Auvenshine*, Pastor of Southside City Church, Fort Worth, TX, and international minister.

I have had the privilege of studying the Bible with Sharon. She has worked hard to gain the knowledge she has and God has used her to make the Bible come alive in my life. I pray that as you do this study God will open your heart and mind and draw you into a closer relationship with Him.—*Suzi Ketch*, Arlington, TX.

I have experienced Sharon's in-depth Bible studies firsthand as a member of a small group which she leads. She has an incredible prayer life in which she seeks God's guidance in all that she does. Her commitment to accuracy in how she handles the Word makes her work trustworthy.—*Jane Matlock*, Burleson, TX.

For Christians seeking spiritual maturity, a knowledgeable teaching hand that provides a fine blend of principle and application is invaluable. Mrs. Gresham has achieved such a blend in this Commentary-Workbook by dissecting the text, interpreting it, connecting it with other Bible texts that enrich it, and, then, by confronting us with sharp questions that make us rethink our Christian lifestyle.—*Loida Pineda*, Director of the School of Music, Seminario Teológico Bautista Mexicano, División Mérida, Mérida Yucatan, Mexico.

With a gift for accurately communicating God's Word in a relevant and personal way, Sharon Gresham's in-depth study of Philippians will delight and thrill any serious student of the Scriptures. I highly recommend it!—*Scott Whitson*, Director of Missions, Southwest Metroplex Baptist Association and former missionary to Tanzania.

Paul's Lifesong

of

Joy *and* Unity

A Commentary-Workbook
Study of the Epistle to the Philippians

SHARON L. GRESHAM

Illustrated by

Svetlin M. Burgudzhiev

WestBow
PRESS
A DIVISION OF THOMAS NELSON

Copyright © 2012 by Sharon L. Gresham.

All rights reserved. No part of this book may be used or reproduced by any means, graphic, electronic, or mechanical, including photocopying, recording, taping or by any information storage retrieval system without the written permission of the publisher except in the case of brief quotations embodied in critical articles and reviews.

© Copyright for the book, Burleson, TX: Sharon L. Gresham, *ASHES TO CROWNS* Ministries, June 2010, April 2011, revised November 2011.

© Copyright for the title "A Commentary-Workbook—A Study of", Burleson, TX: Sharon L. Gresham, *ASHES TO CROWNS* Ministries, November 2011.

© Copyright for the cover designs, Abilene, TX: Svetlin Burgudzhiev. Used by permission of Svetlin Burgudzhiev, December, 2011.

All Hebrew and Greek resources:

For the New Testament (NT) Greek references according to their alphabetized lexical word:

Bauer, *A Greek-English Lexicon of the New Testament*, ed. and trans. William F. Arndt, F. Wilber Gingrich, and Frederick W. Danker, 3rd ed. Chicago: University of Chicago Press, 2000.

For the Hebrew (MT), or Old Testament (OT), references:

The *Brown-Driver-Briggs Hebrew and English Lexicon (BDB)*

Koehler, Ludwig, and Walter Baumgartner, *The Hebrew and Aramaic Lexicon of the Old Testament (KBL)*

All translations belong to this author unless otherwise noted.

WestBow Press books may be ordered through booksellers or by contacting:

WestBow Press
A Division of Thomas Nelson
1663 Liberty Drive
Bloomington, IN 47403
www.westbowpress.com
1-(866) 928-1240

Because of the dynamic nature of the Internet, any web addresses or links contained in this book may have changed since publication and may no longer be valid. The views expressed in this work are solely those of the author and do not necessarily reflect the views of the publisher, and the publisher hereby disclaims any responsibility for them.

Any people depicted in stock imagery provided by Thinkstock are models, and such images are being used for illustrative purposes only.

Certain stock imagery © Thinkstock.

ISBN: 978-1-4497-4583-7 (sc)
ISBN: 978-1-4497-5419-8 (e)

Library of Congress Control Number: 2012907173

Printed in the United States of America

WestBow Press rev. date: 08/29/2012

Table of Contents

Abbreviations vii

Preface ix

Acknowledgments xi

Epigraph xiii

I. Chapter One: A Song of Freedom 1
    A. Introduction: Singing in Prison (1:1-2) 1
        1. Singing a Servant Song 1
        2. Greeting the People 3
    B. The Body of the Letter: Songs of Thanksgiving and Praise (1:3-4:20) 4
        1. Singing with Joy in Prayer for the Philippians 4
        2. Standing Firm in Unity and Joy: Even in Tough Circumstances 12

II. Chapter Two: A Song of Encouragement
for Joy, Unity, and Humility 24
    A. Standing Firm to Sing in Harmony (1:27-2:5) 24
    B. The Christ Hymn: Glorifying and Imitating the Lord (2:6-11) 41
    C. A Continued Song of Obedience (2:12-30) 59
        1. Working with the Lord 59
            a. Love for God 61
            b. Love for People 94
        2. Living in the Light of Life 103
        3. Living as Godly Examples 108

III. Chapter Three: A Song in Minor Key 112
    A. A Modulation from Joy to Woe (3:1) 112
    B. The Song of Woe: The Need for Humility and Hope (3:2-16) 112
    C. A Brighter Song: Realizing Our New Citizenship (3:17-21) 127

IV. Chapter Four: A Call for Songs in Excellent Harmony 132
    A. A Reminder to Stand Firm and Sing in Harmony (4:1) 132
    B. A Dirge against Disunity and Envy: Singing Again in Minor Key (4:2-3) ... 134
    C. The Return to a Major Key (4:4-23) 137
        1. Praising in Every Circumstance, Enjoying the Fruit of Peace 137
        2. Trusting the Lord for Provisions 145
        3. Singing a Song of Farewell 153

Conclusion: A Reminder to Sing 155

My Song of Thanksgiving: An Epilogue 157

About the Author 159

Bibliography 161

Abbreviations

AC	The American Commentary
BAR	*Biblical Archaeology Review*
BDAG	Bauer, *A Greek-English Lexicon of the New Testament*, ed. and trans. William F. Arndt, F. Wilber Gingrich, and Frederick W. Danker, 3rd ed. Chicago: University of Chicago Press, 2000.
BDB	*The Brown-Driver-Briggs Hebrew and English Lexicon*
CBQ	*Catholic Bible Quarterly*
IVPNTC	IVP New Testament Commentary Series
JRE	*Journal of Religious Ethic*
KBL	Koehler, Ludwig, and Walter Baumgartner, *The Hebrew and Aramaic Lexicon of the Old Testament*
KJV	The King James Version
LBC	The Layman's Bible Commentary
LW	*Luther's Works*
NAC	The New American Commentary
NAMB	North American Mission Board
NASU	The New American Standard Bible Updated
NIBC	New International Biblical Commentary
NICNT	The New International Commentary on the New Testament
NIGTC	The New International Greek Testament Commentary
NIV	The New International Version
NovT	*Novum Testamentum*
NTS	Library of New Testament Studies, formerly JSNTSup
PNTC	The Pillar New Testament Commentary
RevExp	*Review and Expositor*
SWBTS	Southwestern Baptist Theological Seminary
TWOT	*Theological Wordbook of the Old Testament*
WBC	Word Biblical Commentary

Preface

This study does not divide into a specific period of time. The material follows more of a verse-by-verse examination of Paul's teachings in the letter to the Philippians. The chapter divisions of this study follow chapters of the biblical text with the exceptions of 1:27-30 and 3:1. Verses 1:27-2:4 flow better together, and 3:1 connects 2:19-30 with the rest of chapter 3. As we inspect these passages, this commentary/Bible study explains why the chapters divide as they do. At times in the study, because of topics within some passages, we will take mini detours (excurses) to study what the Bible says about those issues. Two such excurses involve obedience through love, and envy.

We will investigate the excurses by stepping to the side of some verses and studying the themes they represent. Please stay with me, and we will see why going in those directions is important to understanding Philippians. My prayer is that as you work through the material, you see the continuity for the letter to the Philippians, and that the excurses will add to the study rather than detract from it. The verse-by-verse flow is my reason not to divide this commentary/workbook into a specific timeframe. My prayer is that the Spirit will lead through each verse to enlighten us in what the Lord wants us to understand through the letter to the Philippians.

The theme of this study involves Paul's lifesong which we will glean from many of the verses. Paul looked at life with a joy-filled melody in his heart. We will see his attitude in Philippians, but other Pauline letters confirm his mindset regardless of his circumstances. Some strains of his melody explode with joy in spite of his situations. Other stanzas carry a minor refrain—to teach and warn. As we study the messages of joy and unity in the letter, let's remember that Paul demonstrated his viewpoint while in prison in Philippi (Acts 16), and in prison while writing this letter. He expresses joy and rejoices often.

Please understand that the direction which this study takes is both my interpretation and that of a commentary approach. I believe we all can understand God's Word more deeply and that the Lord wants us to know Him as personally as possible. I do not want to come across as harsh or egotistical—that would violate the very thing Paul wants us to see in the letter. I hope I do not seem legalistic.

I confess that I feel all of us can do much more in learning about God and His Word. I believe we have a *privilege* and *responsibility* to learn and grow as part of the Body of Christ, to encourage each other to go more in-depth in our knowledge of the Word, and to prompt each other to display love and good deeds. That is why I have included other writers' thoughts, not just my interpretation. I want to encourage further investigation into what church leaders and theological professors have written. Their works have blessed me and helped me to grow in my relationship with Jesus Christ.

May the Lord bless and grow you as you study.

Sharon L. Gresham
ASHES TO CROWNS Ministries

Acknowledgments

My love and gratitude go to the Ladies of the Priscilla Class at Alsbury Baptist Church. Their encouragement and willingness to participate in studying Philippians through this Commentary-Workbook has given me wonderful support. Like Priscilla, their passion for the Scriptures, desire for depth of knowledge and truth, and love for missions have blessed me beyond words. They field-tested this work. Their comments and discussion brought changes and corrections to context and content. I love and thank them all.

Epigraph

I thank my God in every mention of you . . . for I am persuaded of *this* thing, that He who has begun a good work in you will bring it to completion up to the day of Christ Jesus (Phil 1:3a, 6).

Chapter One

A Song of Freedom

Introduction: Singing in Prison (1:1-2)

Let's begin by looking at the background of this letter—in other words—the letter in its historical context.

In one sitting, completely read Acts 16 and the letter to the Philippians before going further into this study.

What attitude and actions can we see in Acts 16:11-15, 23-34?

Although Paul and Silas were prisoners and although they were "in bonds," they were not in bondage. Even after being beaten severely, thrown into an inner prison, and their feet placed in stocks—seemingly with no chance of escape—they burst into songs of praise. They prayed to the Lord whom they trusted to set them free. If they stayed imprisoned, faced death, or suffered more, they believed God would take care of them.

God heard the songs of Paul and Silas and chose to intervene. He set them free. But then, they already were free in Christ—that was what had them singing!

The people imprisoning Paul were the ones in bondage: to financial and political gain, and to sin. Still, in verse 1 Paul says he is a slave. Let's look at the bonds Paul, Silas, and Timothy chose to accept.

Singing a Servant Song

Philippians 1:1a. Paul and Timothy, bond-servants of Christ Jesus, to all the saints (believers, Christians) in Christ Jesus

Paul usually began his letters by stating the names of the people with him. Timothy was with him when Paul wrote Philippians. Timothy was not necessarily writing the letter as Paul's secretary, or adding to what Paul said; Timothy just sent his greetings.

In Philippians 1:1a, Paul identifies himself and declares his authority to write the letter. We might wonder how Paul could say he has authority when he says he is a *servant*. Servants do not usually have rights. As we will see, the issue of servanthood is predominant in this letter for everyone. We will see as we go further that Paul points to Christ Jesus as the ultimate example of being a servant, and the Lord certainly has authority. Let's see what Paul means by being a servant.

Paul implies that he and Timothy are a type of slave: a *voluntary bond-servant* of Jesus.

    a. Paul uses the name "bond-servants" as if renaming himself and Timothy. He gives what is known as an appositive—another name. Paul is saying, "You can rename us 'the slaves of Christ.'"

    b. We may not fully understand the idea of *volunteering* to be a slave. A slave totally belongs to the owner. We need to grasp the meaning as being *completely sold out to Jesus Christ as Master*.

    c. The OT provides a vivid illustration of how bond-servants could choose to bind themselves to someone.

Read Exodus 21:1-6. How does binding in this way affect how we should live as servants of Christ?

As Jews who knew the Hebrew Scriptures, Paul and Timothy would understand this concept of a bondservant (Phil 3:4-6; 2 Tim 1:3-6; 3:14-15). They have chosen to bind themselves to Christ spiritually like the slaves in Exodus 21:1-6. These two men see themselves as leaders who are chosen by the Lord—to be servants. This view teaches humility in servanthood for Christ, but also carries an important OT teaching about authority.

Read the following passages. Beside each passage, name the leader and what God calls that person:

Deuteronomy 34:5:	Jeremiah 33:21:
Psalm 105:26:	Ezekiel 37:25:
Psalm 105:42:	Amos 3:7:
Judges 2:8:	Zechariah 1:6:
2 Samuel 7:5:	

In these verses God describes the OT leaders of the nation of Israel as His servants. The tradition, which the NT writers would understand, indicates these leaders had authority. Through God's appointing them as leaders, they had the ability to speak for God.

At the same time, the leaders realized their humble position with the Lord. They served Him through serving others. The NT leaders were pointing to their God-given place, but doing it with awareness of serving humbly alongside other people.[1]

Read John 13, 17, and 19. How did Christ demonstrate His servant leadership?

---

[1]   Ben Witherington III, *Paul's Letter to the Romans; A Socio-Rhetorical Commentary* (Grand Rapids: William B. Eerdmans Publishing, 2004), 30-31; Douglas J. Moo, *The Letter of James*, PNTC, ed. D. A. Carson (Grand Rapids: William B. Eerdmans Publishing, 2000), 48.

We will see throughout the letter that Paul refers to Christ's servanthood as the model to emulate. Paul writes this letter from another prison; he has been imprisoned for his faith in Christ in Rome.

Greeting the People

Philippians 1:1b. To all the saints who are in Philippi:

In the first two verses, Paul identifies his audience—the recipients of his letter. Philippi was a region conquered by Greece and named after Philip, the father of Alexander the Great. Philip was born in this area. When the Romans took over the region, they gave the people citizenship which offered freedom from taxes and harsh rule.[2] Paul visited Philippi on his second and third missionary journeys.

At this point, in the back of your Bible or on a computer, find the map(s) of Paul's missionary journeys. The map can show where Philippi was and the relationship of Macedonia to other places to which Paul wrote letters. Take a few minutes to see where Philippi was in relationship to Rome and other major Empire cities such as Ephesus and Corinth.

Later in this study we will see why some of these places and their relationship to Rome mattered to the Philippian church members. Those relationships influenced the reason, or occasion, for the letter.

Philippians 1:1c. (To all the saints) including the overseers (bishops, pastors) and deacons:

Saints represent *believers*. Paul indicates that all Christians are set apart at conversion and are saints. The term, *saints*, also can be a synonym for the church.

Paul involves the local leadership when he addresses the church. He calls the leaders *overseers* and *deacons*. Even though he founded the church at Philippi (Acts 16) and other churches in Macedonia, he could not be the pastor for all of them. He was a church planter: someone who began churches. He stayed in touch with the people the best way he could—through letters and people who came to see him. He left local people as leaders to guide the churches. Luke (Acts 16:16), Lydia (Acts 16:14-15, 40), Euodia and Syntyche (Phil 4:2-3) and Clement (Phil 4:3) possibly were the initial leaders in the church at Philippi.

Through this letter Paul deals with specific issues that are happening in the church in Philippi. He does expect the letter to circulate to other churches in Macedonia to help with similar situations. Paul encourages the leadership and the laypeople to change where they should and to remain firm in what they are doing correctly.

---

2   Michael J. Gorman, *Apostle of the Crucified Lord: A Theological Introduction to Paul and His Letters* (Grand Rapids: William B. Eerdmans Publishing, 2004), 48-49.

Philippians 1:2. Grace to you and peace from God our Father and the Lord Jesus Christ.

Paul gives a normal greeting here such as he did in most of his letters. The greeting implies a blessing to the recipients. Paul recognizes how God has given him grace by saving him. Paul wants his readers to experience God's grace and peace as well. The book of Philippians is one of the most positive and upbeat epistles Paul wrote.

The Body of the Letter: Songs of Thanksgiving and Praise (1:3-4:20)

Singing with Joy in Prayer for the Philippians

In 2002, I had the privilege of singing with The Singing Churchwomen of Oklahoma. One of the songs we sang was written by Cindy Berry. She wrote the song from Philippians 1:3-5. Cindy has a way of taking the singer and listener to the heights of delight through her music. We were singing praises to the Lord by singing His words back to Him and sharing those words with others. I wonder if Paul might have been humming as he wrote the following prayer. He grounded the prayer in his thanksgiving and praise to the Lord for the Philippians. I cannot read verses 3-5 without Cindy's song sending me soaring again.

Philippians 1:3. I thank my God in all my remembrance of you,

As Paul did for his readers, I thank God for you and your willingness to allow me to lead you in this Bible study. My heart's desire is to study the Word of God in depth in order to learn what God originally intended in the original contexts for life, worship, and needs of the community. In that way, we can apply His word appropriately to our lives today.

Philippians 1:4. always offering prayer with joy in my every prayer for you all,

As you study this material, consider studying it in a group. Take time to get to know one another as much as possible. Anticipate the joy that grows by identifying with each other in prayer. I encourage that you create two charts:

The first one could include your names, contact information, and interesting things you may not know about each other.

The second one would be a Prayer/Praise Journal Table. Include five columns: Date of the Request, Medical Issues, Salvation and Christian Growth, Other Needs, and the Date of God's Answer (Praise).

As you study together, I hope you will embrace Paul's methods of praising and praying *in joy* for others.

From this point forward, when you encounter the Scripture address in bold print, please turn to that passage in your Bible. When I discuss passages or give interpretations, I have translated the passages from the Greek and Hebrew, so your version may be slightly different from mine. If I quote a verse from other versions, I will indicate that version.

Philippians 1:5. Literally, the verse says, "sharing in the *koinonia* in the gospel" (italics mine). The word *koinonia* is the word we usually translate as *fellowship, participation*, or *close relationship*.

List as many ways as possible that your study group, Sunday school class, Bible study group, or church can participate or associate in the *fellowship/participation* of the gospel?

Philippians 1:6. What does Paul say about our journey with Christ?

Acts 9 tells the story about how Jesus and Paul met, how Jesus saved Paul from sin (*justification*), and how He called Paul as an apostle. Paul became convinced (*persuaded, won over*) that Jesus was the Messiah. By the time he wrote this letter, Paul was confident that Jesus began the relationship and would continue to make Paul into the child of God the apostle needed to be. This process is what we call *sanctification*, our growth in our relationship with Jesus Christ. The literal translation of Philippians 1:6 is, "For I am fully persuaded of this thing, that He who has begun a good work in you will bring it to completion up to the day of Christ Jesus."

We owe our very being to Christ. Not only do we owe our lives to Him, but we also owe Him the credit of giving us a very personal relationship with Him. Christ started everything—as Creator and as Savior. He, who *made the very beginnings* of everything, initiated life.

After reading the following verses, tell what kind of life Christ gives us:

John 10:10:   2 Peter 1:2-4:

1 Peter 1:3-5:   2 Peter 1:5-8; Galatians 5:22-23:

1 Peter 2:9:

Now read Ephesians 1:3-6. *How* did God set up the relationship so we could know Him?

When did God determine that we could know Him and be in relationship with Him?

What God started before He created the world, He will continue until Christ comes to take us home to heaven. We can be encouraged even though it seems He takes a long time to work in our lives. He is working on our maturity. My prayer is that He is able to work on me in such a way that the closer I get to heaven, the more like Christ I am, and God will not have to change me a lot when I get there. Paul wants to encourage the people that what God starts, He completes. Paul also reassures the people that he enjoys being a part of their growth.

Philippians 1:7. What kind of relationship does Paul have with the Philippians?

Identify the three elements in this verse that tell of Paul's and the Macedonians' relationship:

1.
2.
3.

Paul says it is right for him—as a moral obligation—to *have them in mind, be intent on, set his mind on* them in a special way. Paul *loves* these people. His affection is deep! In the *defense and confirmation* of the gospel, the Philippians were one of the few groups who helped him—and helped him without strings attached.

The churches in Macedonia supported Paul's ministry even while Paul was in prison. They gave more than their money; they gave of themselves, as we will see in chapter 3. Paul and the Philippians demonstrate that relationships with others must have this kind of heart-felt emotion so the gospel spreads. The way people grow in Christ can depend on how we think and act towards them.

The verb *to think* in the first part of this verse means Paul had developed a special mindset about these people. That outlook included warm opinions and viewpoints about them. He had a particular reason to encourage them to continue doing all the right things they had already been doing.

Read Romans 8:5-9. What does this say about the proper outlook?

Read Romans 12:1-2. What are we to do with our mindset?

Read Colossians 3:1-5. What did Paul say we should do to get the proper attitude?

What do these three passages have to do with Paul's attitude towards the Philippians?

Paul will speak of this mindset ten times in Philippians. The key to our attitude is tied to Christ's viewpoint about people and circumstances. We will see how Paul lives with this outlook even in adversity.

The people of Macedonia helped Paul spread the gospel. Read Acts 16:11-15. How did Lydia help?

Read Acts 16:40. What did the church do to participate?

Read Philippians 4:10-18. How did Paul feel about the church's gift?

From the beginning of Paul's ministry in Philippi, the Macedonians wanted to help him. After he left, some new people had become part of the church. They did not want to follow Paul's leadership. They were delighted that Paul was in prison again. Those people opposed Paul's leadership, because they did not consider Paul an apostle and did not want to help him.

Read 2 Corinthians 8:1-11. Contrast the two mindsets towards helping. What are the two attitudes and to whom do they belong?

What causes the differences in those attitudes?

Read the following five verses. What is the difference in the appositives Paul gives in these greetings?

1 Corinthians 1:1:
2 Corinthians 1:1:
Galatians 1:1:
Ephesians 1:1:
Philippians 1:1:

We saw from the appositive in Philippians 1:1 that Paul did not have to defend his apostleship to the majority of the church. Most of the people did not care if he were in prison; they wanted to help him. They saw his imprisonment as an opportunity to aid their church planter and help him continue to spread the gospel.

Throughout the letter of Philippians we will see how our attitudes towards others reflect on our relationship with the Lord's work. The mindset we develop even towards one individual in the church can impact our witness with others in the home, church, and workplace.

When have you experienced a time that your mindset helped the spread of the gospel?

When did an attitude hinder the gospel?

Philippians 1:8-11. Does Paul seem presumptuous to claim God as his witness? Why or why not?

Paul does not contradict God's Word about appealing to God's name in an oath. Paul knows that God is willing to put His holy reputation on the line for His believers. The Lord's Spirit would testify that Paul longs for the people of Macedonia, and longs to see people come to Christ as Lord.

In the Old Testament (OT) God required two witnesses in a trial before anyone could be condemned. The person could testify for himself. Therefore, Paul is calling on God to serve as a witness that the apostle has the right affection towards the church members. The Lord can testify that Paul *fervently longs* to be with the church again. The fervor with which Paul *greatly longs* is that *deep affection*.

In Romans 1:11-12, what else does Paul *long* to do?

In Philippians 1:8-11, what drives Paul's passion?

In Romans 1:11, Paul states that he *craved* to share a spiritual gift with them. He yearned that the Romans continue in faith. The passion to share with the Romans is the same passion he felt for the Philippians.

What was Paul's prayer in Philippians—how did he *long* for the people there?

What a way to pray for someone! Paul demonstrates how believers should pray for others. The word for *abound* means to *overflow, to have more than enough*.

In Philippians 1:8-9 Paul uses the words *affection* and *love*. From verse 9, in the section below name the two things love was to involve:

1.
2.

A warning appears here. Paul states that love needs discernment. We all love some people who hurt us. However, love does not mean we have to let them continue to hurt us. Love means solid boundaries. Our love comes from our relationship with Christ. The Lord does not approve inappropriate things being done to people. Knowledge and discernment carry a purpose, a responsibility, not to allow unnecessary hurt.

From Philippians 1:9-11 tell why Paul wants his readers to exhibit real knowledge and discernment.

Why would Paul use the term *real* in reference to knowledge?

In verse 10, we are to *approve*, or *make a critical examination*, of something. What does 1:10 say we are to approve?

Describe how to overflow with *insight* and *thorough discernment*.

What does this tell us about our relationship with the Lord's Spirit?

Paul uses an assaying term here. We are to test or approve what is excellent as deeply as miners analyze ore. The Greek word for excellent means *what is superior*, *what is best*, or *what is worth more than* anything else. Many times have we heard that we are to choose the best over the good. In mining, gold or silver miners sometimes accept lower grade ore, but here the terminology means we are to accept *nothing but* the excellent. We are to use God's insight, discernment, and true knowledge to accept what is worth more spiritually than what the world tells us is okay. The Spirit helps us determine what is best.

Name some things the world tells us are good or all right.

What does this verse encourage you to change?

What do our families or children accept as right which may not be the best for them?

Philippians 1:11. Also read Galatians 5:22-23. Notice *how* we grow in our walk with Jesus. How does verse 11 indicate we possess the fruit of righteousness?

From whom do we get the fruit in Philippians 1:11?

From whom do we get the fruit in Galatians 5:22-23?

Read Galatians 5:19-21. Notice that the word which introduces the vices is plural while the word for fruit is singular. What does Paul call those vices?

Why do you think the Holy Spirit would inspire Paul to use the plural form for *acts* or *works* in Galatians 5:19, but the singular form for *fruit* in 5:22 although several virtues are listed?

The picture here is that the Lord fills us with His qualities as if *paying or delivering* one thing to us. In the Greek, both in Philippians 1:11 and Galatians 5:22-23, the word for fruit is singular—not fruits, but fruit—as one package the Holy Spirit brings into our lives when He comes to live in us.

Consider how the fruit intertwine with Paul's feelings for the believers in Philippi. The connection is twofold:

1. Paul praises the saints in Philippi to encourage their growth *in* living the fruit of righteousness;
2. Paul praises them *for* their fruit of righteousness.

The situation is a both/and. We need to grow in the fruit and use of the fruit. We also should encourage each other to grow in the Lord.

Read Galatians 5:22 again. What is the first verb?

Galatians 5:22-23 says the fruit *is*. The fruit *already* exists in us. Too often people have misrepresented what Christ wants to do in our lives with the fruit. Many of us have heard or said, "Lord, give me patience and I need it right now!" Then we laugh because we think we have asked an oxymoron—*patience now*. We also say "Lord, *teach* me humility."

What is wrong with this kind of thinking?

Read 2 Peter 1:3-4. What does this passage say we have?

I recall sitting in our parsonage on the island of Guam. I was upset about something very inappropriate which had been said to our daughter. I begged God to *teach me* to love that person as I should. I felt as if the Lord were giving me this thought:

"Sharon, why do you ask me to teach you what I have already given you? You have all the love you need. You cannot love that person on your own, but I can love through you. You *have* My fruit of My Spirit. In the same way you possess love, you have all the joy, peace, patience . . . that you need *exactly when* you need it."

God's fruit is for now. He does not want to have to teach us what He has already given us to use. He will put us under His training regimen if we do not appropriate that fruit into our lives, if we do not practice the fruit in daily situations. *We do grow* in our understanding and use of the fruit. However, we can cry to the Lord at any moment for any of the fruit we need. We already have each part in our lives.

If you have trouble needing patience, ask the Lord to be patient through you right at that time. Accept His patience at the very moment you need it. You may not "feel" patient, but the Lord will work patience in and through you.

When we lived in southern California, friends with Campus Crusade for Christ taught me the practice of spiritual breathing: Pray as you inhale the quality of each piece of the fruit and exhale the problem. For instance, "Lord, I breathe in your love and breathe out my hatred (animosity). I inhale your joy as I exhale my unhappiness . . ."[3]

Do you have hate, anger, fear, impatience, a lack of self-control, etc.?

Pray in the fruit and pray out the vice. Write how praying this way changed your thoughts concerning the fruit:

Since we already have the fruit, this exercise puts the focus in the right place. We seek the most excellent thing: God's fruit of righteousness rather than our vices. The Lord has given us the fruit for a reason.

Reread Philippians 1:11. Why do we get the fruit?

Our lives infused with the fruit of righteousness can deliver praise and glory to God. God receives glory because of what Christ has begun and continues to do in us. Throughout Paul's writings about the fruit (Phil 1:10-11; Gal 5:22-23), he points to the Father, Son, and Holy Spirit as givers of the fruit, of doing the same things.

Why would Paul indicate the Father, Son, and Spirit do the same things?

We know the Father, Son, and Spirit as the Trinity. Paul uses all three Persons in his letters. Although the word *Trinity* is not in the Bible, we see the doctrine of the Trinity throughout the biblical text. The church did not name the doctrine until the Council of Nicea in 325 A.D. The leaders based this teaching on what they realized the Hebrew Scriptures (First Testament) and the New (Second) Testament dictated.

Let me mention a little aside here. The Old Testament was the First Testament written. The Old is not old, just first. God's Word in the First Testament is still alive. We understand it both

---

[3]   Used by permission from Campus Crusade for Christ (January 27, 2012).

because God still speaks to us through that inspired document, and also through the light the New sheds on it. Therefore, we see the Trinity in both Testaments.

When we recognize that the Son gives us the fruit of righteousness, we know the Spirit and Father are working at the same time. When the Father works, the Son and Spirit work. When the Spirit works, the Father and Son also work. The Three Persons of the Trinity are never divided, because they are the One God.

The word that expresses their working together—at the same time—is *perichoresis*. The perichoresis refers to the inter-working, the *inter-participation*, of the Trinity. What the Trinity began before the foundation of the world, Christ completed through the cross event, and the indwelling Spirit continues to work into our lives. The Spirit's fruit and purpose continue until the day Christ comes again.

Paul exhorts in this letter that all is done for the glory and praise of God (1:11). The word for glory is *doxa*. We get the word *doxology* from it. The term *-ology* usually means *the study of* . . . We have the privilege of participating in the study and practice of the glory of God.

We can give glory without singing. Giving the Lord glory involves the practice of worship with our everyday lives. *Everything we do in life is worship.* We can worship badly or well. By approving the things that are excellent, we worship well, daily. However, in worshipping well, don't we really have a song in our hearts just as Paul did?

We can choose what is superior in every situation, because we have the fruit of the Spirit. We live to the glory of God. We live to offer the doxology of our very lives to the Lord.

Standing Firm in Unity and Joy: Even in Tough Circumstances

Philippians 1:12. What was Paul's attitude about the circumstances of his life?

Are you willing to look at your circumstances—the hurts of your past or the hardships of your life now—with the attitude that the difficulties help the advancement of the gospel?

Are you willing to allow the circumstances of your life to grow you and grow others in Christ?

How do you feel about looking at the hurts and hardships in this way?

Reread Philippians 1:3-12.

Paul looked at his imprisonment and his dependence on others with such joy that people could see the Lord in the circumstances and in his life.

Philippians 1:13. The result of Paul's imprisonment is twofold. What results has Paul mentioned?

1.

2.

The Praetorian Guard knew why Paul was imprisoned. As many of them served their shift with him, he would evangelize them—share the gospel of Christ with them. They would talk among themselves about Paul's being under house-arrest because of his beliefs. As a result, Caesar's palace was affected by Christ, even though Caesar considered himself a god.

Almighty God determined to reach the most people with the gospel regardless of where Paul was. While Paul was under house-arrest, visitors could come to see him. Apparently many people came. The Philippian church supported him and the Rome church was encouraged by his life.

Philippians 1:14. What do you do in times of trial?

What is your attitude when things go wrong or are hard to handle?

How did Paul's reaction affect others?

How are you encouraged when you see other people going through trials?

Philippians 1:15-18e. What does Paul think of his chains?

Since Paul considers that his chains come from the Lord, he can rejoice. People are trusting the Lord and believers are speaking about Jesus with boldness which they did not have previously. Although some proclaim Christ to receive attention like Paul is getting, he will rejoice that they are preaching the gospel too.

Does rejoicing mean we should not grieve in our circumstances?

Paul certainly would not have liked the inability to preach freely from place to place. Because of his passion to share the gospel, he might have grieved that he could not begin other churches. He surely longed to tell people what Christ had done for him. Paul would understand, though, that his ordeal could mean the gospel would also be on trial. He knew that his attitudes and actions could determine whether the gospel would be accepted.

Regardless of our circumstance, we are to share Christ with others. Sharing may mean living in such a way that during our hardships people will want to know the Lord who gives us joy. We may need to allow people to see us grieve our difficulties so they are free to grieve, but they still need to see Christ through our difficulties.

Notice in 1:15 the reaction of those preaching from envy and selfish motives. They could be the kind of people who love to kick someone while that person is down. This group did not participate in the gospel the way Paul wanted, but Paul was still thrilled the gospel was preached.

When someone is down, do you judge them?

How do you react to a person who is hurt?

Paul's perspective could allow him to see each situation as one in which the gospel could be preached. He would refuse to be upset because people were not preaching with the attitude they should. The message about Christ is the good news that had to be shared.

How do you practice Paul's perspective?

How can you share the good news in your situation?

What must you do first before you can be an effective witness in your situation?

Notice the group that preached with pure motives. Paul rejoices that most in the Roman church have shared the gospel out of love. The word translated "pure motives" in some English versions is the Greek word for love: *agape*. The KJV has translated this more closely. Most of the Roman Christians have helped spread the gospel in love—that gives Paul another reason to rejoice—the love the believers have for Christ! This group realized that since Paul could no longer work as he desired, they could fill the gap. The people did what Paul could not do. Their actions show they lived what he taught.

Read Romans 1:14-17. What lessons did the Roman church learn about helping Paul?

Read Romans 4:4-8. What in these verses gives a hint about Paul's life?

Read Romans 5:1-8. What does Paul say about what we should do in our circumstances?

Why does Paul believe we should feel this way?

What do we have that gives us the ability to feel and act as Paul suggests?

Read through Romans 8. Beginning in verse 1, list verses from the chapter that uplift and encourage you right now, and give you hope no matter what you are experiencing. Beside each verse, tell why the verse encourages you.

Philippians 1:18f-20. In verses 18f-20 Paul lists three things he knows. In the section below, state them:

1.
2.
3.

List two things that have given Paul assurance of what he knows:

1.
2.

We see in Philippians 1:18d-20 that Paul refuses to stop rejoicing just because peoples' motives are not right. He plans to rejoice that:

a.   the Philippians pray;
b.   they provide for his needs;
c.   he expects the emperor will release him from the death sentence.

Read Job 13:15-16. What does Job say will happen?

In Philippians 1:19, Paul expresses a similar hope like Job's from the Greek Old Testament (the Septuagint or LXX). Paul says, "I know this will turn out for my deliverance."

Read Psalm 34:3-6 and 35:37. What do Job, the Psalmists, and Paul tell us about troubles and trials?

Paul tells us in 1:18-20 that he expects God to deliver him from death or from hell. Paul would rejoice in either of those decisions. He really anticipated that the Lord would release him from prison and imminent death. He realized that other people needed to hear the gospel.

If he had to die, Paul knew the Father would not let him be disgraced for worshipping Jesus. He could give his final, bold witness for the gospel, and the Lord would take him to heaven.[4] Regardless of the way God would deliver Paul, the Lord would vindicate him.

Deliverance implies *vindication*. For Paul, both life and death would point to his relationship with Jesus. Either way, Paul would demonstrate that it was worth his life to serve Christ.

When has the Lord vindicated you for worshipping and serving Him?

Did you have that hope, that *earnest expectation*, for God's intervention which Paul expresses?

Did you sense the Spirit working both in you and in the situation?

What hope do you have that He will continue to do so?

Read Romans 5:8. Why can we expect God's hope in our difficult situations?

Can you rejoice like Paul?

Read Psalm 69:22-28. Did you try to *help God* with His deliverance?

When people need vindication, how do you pray for them so the Spirit provides them earnest expectation and hope?

Take time and write a letter to the Lord thanking Him for His vindication, His hope in your situation, and His Spirit in you.

The Christians in Philippi have prayed for Paul and helped with his needs (Phil 1:19), but the Holy Spirit supplies Paul with Himself—partly in response to those prayers. Paul wants to stand boldly for Christ, and the Spirit—the indwelling Christ—understands Paul's desire to honor the Lord. The Spirit provides that ability so Paul will not be ashamed of anything in his walk with the Lord, not even his imprisonment. The humble piety Paul exhibits comes from his trust in God. God would provide the power and deliverance, whatever that deliverance might be, so Paul could exalt Christ in every way possible.

---

4   Fee, *Paul's Letter to the Philippians*, 42-43.

Read Malachi 3:1-3. What do we see in the prophecy of the Lord?

What role does the Lord play in these verses?

How do the verses apply to our circumstances?

You may have heard the illustration about the silversmith.[5] In order to burn off the impure matter around the metal, he has to heat the metal with extremely high temperatures. The fire is so hot that the silversmith can look into the molten metal. He wants to see his image reflected in the liquid. When he cannot see himself, he increases the heat. The fire of God cleanses us of the filth in our lives so we reflect the image of God.

The 19th century priest Monsignor Landriot wrote a book about the filling of the Holy Spirit. He believed that the Holy Spirit's fire softens us to cleanse us, but also *hardens* us.[6] Our hearts have to be free of filth for Holy God to see Himself clearly. While the fire softens, it hardens.

God wants to solidify His teaching in us—as Romans 5:3-5 mentions—so we possess strength to stand for the Lord. Jesus Christ can soften and cleanse us during trials. However, the Lord also develops firmness within us which we did not display before each trial. Paul wants his readers to recognize firmness in their lives when trials come.

We generally do stand taller, straighter, and cleaner after the hard times. The filth no longer weighs us down. Confirmation of God's presence becomes clearer. We have the strength to stand firm for the Lord.

As we move more towards an attitude such as Paul's, we can thank the Lord for His work in our lives—for cleansing *and* hardening. Such developments produce a stronger character. That character builds the desired proper attitude.

We cannot display arrogance about God's strengthening us. We must recognize that God has solidified us as "the consistency of marble ... with the shape more sharply defined," "without losing the pliability of charity."[7] Shaping conforms us to the image of Christ.

In the act of hardening, "the soul will have suffered one of the most painful, but most merciful operations of the Holy Spirit."[8] Personally, I find the burning and hardening concepts difficult *even though* encouraging. The encouragement brings the joy Paul preaches and lives.

Do these thoughts help you or intimidate you?   Why?

In what area of your life do you need victory, burning, or hardening?

---

[5]   The author is unknown.

[6]   Monsignor Landriot, *Conferences on the Holy Spirit*, trans. by T. T Carter (Oxford: A. R. Mowbray and Company, 1899), 121-145.

[7]   Ibid., 140, 142.

[8]   Ibid., 142.

Read 2 Corinthians 2:14-17. List two actions Christ is doing for and in us.

1.
2.

Can you view your situation as if you already are a victor because Christ has won the victory?   Why or why not?

What aroma do you think you portray to God?

　　　　　To the world?

What is the reason we can be a positive aroma to God?

This week when the trials of life come, the struggles make you feel as though you lose, and the difficulties around you stink, remember—because of Christ—you are a wonderful, fragrant aroma to God and the world.

This discussion reminds me of one of our grandsons when he was a baby. With acid reflux, he would constantly spit up. On days when he did not lose his breakfast, lunch, or snacks, he smelled pretty good. Still, even on days when he smelled like spit-up, he was refreshment to me. He was my grandson.

You are God's child because of Jesus. You do not stink to Him. You are precious to Him.

We need to remember that we are on a journey. God works His truths into our lives. We can grip onto His promises and commit to letting God lead us in triumph. That is how we are sweet-smelling to the Lord.

At the time of this writing, my new friend Jan Moses had a tough but glorious walk through cancer. We saw beautiful faith in her life. I received emails from her that helped me know how to pray specifically for her and to know where she was in her journey. The letter below shows her disappointments. The cleansing fire of testing comes through this letter, but so do the hardening and strengthening of her faith. Jan knew what the song of life meant just as Paul did:

God Will Make a Way

God is serious about not giving another His glory or His praise to idols (anything that takes the place of God in our lives). I still don't have a *treatment plan* in place—it has now been over 4 months since my last cancer vaccine and 1½ months since I would have received my last vaccine.

Since the last update, I found out about a monoclonal antibody clinical trial (the new "wave" of treatment for melanoma) in Dallas that my local oncologist and the prior clinical trial doctor all felt would be good for me since it targets the immune system.

I interviewed with the new trial, but when the doctors discussed my case, they felt that it would not be suitable for me. So I am still seeking, still praying, still asking. It has been a stressful 2 weeks. The orthopedic oncologist finally talked to the MD Anderson oncologist about the **hip biopsy** – 3 days AFTER my gallbladder surgery. He was willing to work me in for surgery last week, but my surgeon didn't think that I needed to have another surgery so soon, especially since it would be an open incision and not needle biopsy. (More possibilities of problems.) So that biopsy is on hold. But praise God that the hip is feeling better; I think because I have seen a lymph drainage therapist. It seems that the pain is related to swelling – a side effect of the radiation and surgery.

Never have I felt so desperately in need of God's direction. Yes, it has been discouraging; I have felt tempted to just give up the effort to search for treatment. At the same time, I know that God is in control and in His timing, He will show me the right thing to do. I talk to people who get our updates and they think that I never get down. No, I have my moments. But I go back again to God's Word which is TRUTH—not the discouraging lies of the enemy, not the dismal statistics of the cancer doctors, not just "thinking positive thoughts" philosophy. God's Word gets me focused again on Jesus, the author and perfecter of our faith. His promises reassure me, comfort me, challenge me, calm me.

Let me show you how God did that this past week. I woke Tuesday with the song "**God will make a way**" going through my head. Maybe this is how Zephaniah 3:17 is true in my life—"*The Lord your God **is with you**, He is mighty to save. He will take great delight in you, He will quiet you with His love, **He will rejoice over you with singing**.*"

Often the praise songs that we sing are based on Scripture (it is His word, so God does sing to us through them). Using this song, I looked up Scripture references to it. I knew that Isaiah 43 had references to roads in the wilderness so I started there. As I read through the Word, then I dialogued (sometimes with tears) with God over it – asking and answering questions. God says, "*Forget the former things; do not dwell on the past.* (Past treatment?) *See I am doing a **new** thing! Now it springs up; do you not perceive it? (Is. 43:19)*" I responded, "No, Lord, I don't see yet what you are doing or what direction I am to take." God continues, "*I am making a way in the desert and streams in the wasteland* (for what purpose, God?)... *to give drink to my people, my chosen, the people I formed for myself that they may proclaim my praise.*" (Is. 43:20-21)

God reminded me anew of His purpose for me in this cancer journey – to proclaim His praise, to show forth His glory. Here are the other Scriptures that comforted me and set my feet firmly back on the Rock:

God will make a way
Where there seems to be no way.
He works in ways we cannot see;
He will make a way for me.

"My ways are not your ways, declares the Lord. I will tell you of new things, of **hidden things** unknown to you. **No eye has seen**,… no mind has conceived what God has prepared for those who love Him." (Is 55:8; Is 48:6; 1 Cor 2:9)

He will be my guide,
Hold me closely to His side.
With love and strength for each new day,
     He will make a way.
     God will make a way.

"He will be **my guide** even to the end. The Lord stood at **my side** and gave me **strength**. O LORD, we long for you. Be our strength **every morning**. In all their distress, He too was distressed…**In His love** and mercy He redeemed them; He lifted them up and carried them all the days of old. It is God who arms me with strength and makes **my way** perfect." (Ps. 48:14; 2 Tim. 4:17; Is. 33:2; Is 63:9; Ps. 18:32)

By a roadway in the wilderness He leads me.
And rivers in the desert will I see.
Heaven and earth will fade.
But His Word will still remain.
And He will do something new today.

"Some wandered in desert wastelands…The **LORD led them** by a straight way. I will make **rivers flow** on barren heights…so that people may see and know that the hand of the LORD has done this. In the beginning you laid the foundations of the earth, and the heavens are the work of your hand. They will perish, but you will remain. The **Word of our God** stands forever." (Ps. 107:4; Is. 41:18, 20; Ps. 102:25; Is. 40:8)

God will make a way
Where there seems to be no way.
He works in ways we cannot see;
He will make a way for me.

"The highway in the wilderness will be called the way of Holiness… the redeemed will enter Zion with singing; …gladness and joy will overtake them, and sorrow and sighing will flee away. Whether you turn to the right or to the left, you will hear a voice behind you, saying, 'This is the way; walk in it." (Is. 35: 8-10; Is 30:21)

He will be my guide,
Hold me closely to His side.

With love and strength for each new day,   He will make a way.
   God will make a way. Walking in His way,
   Jan[9]

Thank you for letting me share part of Jan's journey with you. If you have experienced the illness of a loved one, or have gone through sicknesses yourself, *by no means* do I want to add guilt to your grief if perhaps you have struggled differently.

We all grieve in diverse ways. Grief is God's gift. We are to mourn with each other. Therefore I want you to know as I write this, I am hurting—for our loss—but also because I do not want to cause hurt for you as you read this example.

[As I originally wrote this section, we lost Jan and two other friends to cancer—within two months. I also went through a very difficult time in my own life. I hit bottom with grief. I had to get alone at a retreat center just to work through my emotions, my anxiety about my future studies some of which had been ripped from me, and my need to be available to help my friends in their hurt. All of these friends were precious, godly, strong people, and I ached for them.]

The Priscilla class has gone through this study as I have written it, and has walked Jan's and the others' journeys with me. Jan's and her family's faith and the other friends' attitudes, have buoyed our faith. The strength of Jan, the two friends, and their families have testified to the way Paul says we are to handle our difficulties.

Therefore can we echo with Jan, Paul, and others what verse 21 says? Read it next.

Philippians 1:21. What does your life say to others?

Paul tells us in verse 21 that to live is Christ; Jan Moses reflected this teaching. The Greek word for *to live* indicates the *process* of living.[10] When the apostle says that living is Christ, he points to how Christ is the only significance.[11] Paul's whole focus has been on Christ. Dying actually would be better, for Paul would be in heaven with Jesus. Still, more work needed to be done on earth.

If you had to choose between heaven and earth *right now*, which do you think you would choose and why?

None of us wants to endure the pain of suffering. To desire to be with the Lord is not a cop-out or a sign of weakness when we are in pain. Paul knew if he were to die, he would face the horror of

---

[9]   Jan Moses, an unpublished email; Mark Moses, *An Uncommon Faith: The Story of Missionary Jan Moses and Her Journey with Cancer* (Garland, TX: Hannibal Books, 2007), 155-58. Used by permission from Mark Moses. The song appears in the published book.

[10]   Gerald F. Hawthorne, *Philippians*, WBC 43, ed. Bruce M. Metzger, Ralph P. Martin, and Lynn Allan Losie (Waco: Word Books, 1983), 45-46.

[11]   Fee, *Paul's Letter to the Philippians*, 140-141.

Rome's methods. He already had faced severely harsh things. If he lived he probably would suffer even more. Yet we will see in chapter 3 just what Paul says about suffering with Christ.

Philippians 1:22-23. You may have heard this story, but it fits here:

"One night the Lord visited a rich man and told him he would die soon. The man was to get his affairs in order. The Lord reminded the man that he could not take any of his riches with him. The man thought a minute and then said, "But Lord, would You mind terribly if I brought just one sack of gold with me?"

The Lord said, "You do not need a sack of gold in heaven. I will provide all your needs and desires."

The man said, "I know, but will You please allow me just one sack?—it would comfort me to know I could have it when I die."

The Lord said, "All right. I will allow it."

A little while later, the man died. When he arrived at the gates of heaven, an angel met him. The angel saw the sack and asked, "What is that? Why did you bring it with you?"

The man said, "The Lord told me I could bring a sack of gold with me."

The angel, looking bewildered, said, "Why did you want to bring pavement?"[12]

Read Revelation 21. What do you see about the home we will have with Jesus?

What makes us cling to this world and the things we have here when we can anticipate all that awaits us?

Someone once asked if this world is not our home (Heb 11:9-10), why we continue to get comfortable here. Paul knew heaven was far better, better than the gold pavement on which he would walk. He wanted to see the Lord and heaven again.

Read 2 Corinthians 12:1-9. What happened to Paul?

Paul knew the Lord's presence and the view were beyond description. At the same time, Paul also knew if he stayed on earth, the Lord would use him to help others. Paul was ready to do both. The dilemma Paul mentions, *I am hard-pressed*, indicates Paul felt *hemmed in on all sides*.[13]

Are you ready to live so close to the Lord, that if He calls you home or if you stay here, you will glorify Him?   Explain your answer.

---

12   Public domain. I heard the story at a ladies' retreat in the form I presented it here.
13   Hawthorne, *Philippians*, 46-47.

Reread Philippians 1:6. List areas of your life where you know God wants to work to make you more like Christ.

Jan mentions in her letter that she still has people with whom she needs to witness. With whom do you need to witness?

Philippians 1:24-26. Who needs you to remain here on earth?

With whom do you still need to share the joy of growing faith?

What other things do you still need to do?

On the other hand, do you see yourself as indispensable, or have you run the race so well that someone else could continue your work if the Lord were to take you home?

Chapter Two

A Song of Encouragement for Joy, Unity, and Humility

Many commentators connect Philippians 1:27-30 as a pericope (selection) with 2:1-5. The verses deal with standing together and showing unity with other people. Since no paragraph division markers existed in the original and earliest Greek manuscripts, we can take 1:27-2:11 together and not hurt our study. In fact, the combination of 1:27-30 with 2:1-5 increases our understanding of 2:6-11. If nothing else, verses 27-30 work as the bridge from 1:3-26 to 2:1.

Standing Firm to Sing in Harmony (1:27-2:5)

Philippians 1:27. When we want our children to listen to us, we may declare, "If you don't hear anything else I say, listen to this …" Paul transitions from praise for God's grace (1:26) to his hopes for the future.

Paul indicates that what he is about to say is of utmost importance. His words are indispensable. Paul is not implying that people disregard anything else he says. However, he wants his readers to conform to the instructions that follow.

We are to conduct ourselves in a manner worthy of the gospel of Christ. The gospel is our *lifestyle*. The Greek word for *conduct* is in command form. It means *be citizens* or *exercise your citizenship*. The only other place Paul uses the verb "conduct" is Acts 23:1.

Read Acts 23:1. How did Paul say he had *exercised his citizenship*?

Read Philippians 3:20, Paul uses the noun form to speak of citizenship. Where is the citizenship of which Paul speaks?

How could you have improved exercising your conduct or citizenship this week?

In Philippians 1:27, Paul expresses that the members should "exercise citizenship." As Roman citizens, the believers would comprehend their duty to stand firm with their neighbors in defense of their country. The members should exercise a similar harmony for the sake of the gospel. Their way of life would illustrate whether they believed Christ was worthy of their lives. They should behave as citizens to two "countries." If they were willing to exist in harmony with non-believers in society, they certainly should live harmoniously within the church. Equally, we today have the responsibility to act in unity with other believers.

Usually when Paul talks about living a worthy life, he uses a different Greek word. That word refers to the *walk* of the Christian. From the following passages we can see how we are to walk.

Read Romans 6:4, 8:4; and, Ephesians 4:1. What words explain our "walk"?

1.
2.
3.

In these verses, the idea is that people walk with Christ in a commendable manner. Whether we walk as individuals or in community, we are to *live* in such a way that the gospel of Christ is not harmed or hindered. We are to stand firm in our conduct. The gospel is not harmed when we stand securely in unity with each other.

In Philippians 1:27, notice two ways Paul says we are to stand firm. What are those two ways?

1.
2.

Does standing firm "in one mind" always mean we agree on everything?

How do we achieve unity?

To be in unity, we each must put our entire life into the process. Paul incorporates *one spirit* and *one mind* to represent a person's will, emotions, and determination. Here the word for *spirit* refers to our spirit. Our spirit must walk *individually* with the Holy Spirit, so our community walks *corporately* in unity.

The word in the Greek for *one mind* literally means *one soul*. We are to use everything inside of us to work towards unity as if all of us possess the very same soul! Our attitudes as individuals and as groups reflect whether the Spirit of Christ directs our thoughts and actions in complete harmony.

In Philippians 1:27, what is the reason or purpose we are to stand firm?

When we *strive* together, the Greek term implies we are fighting beside each other, we are *struggling along with others* to get the job done.[1]

---

[1]   *BDAG*, s. v. συναθλέω.

What is that job?

Read Philippians 4:3 in the New International Version (NIV; if you do not have an NIV but have a computer, you can find a copy online). What word does the NIV use for the same idea?

At the time Paul writes the letter, in this very church two women are *contending* or struggling *against* each other. Instead of standing firm and contending against false teachings and arrogance which have entered the church, instead of helping each other spread the gospel, they are fighting. Paul says they fight from their pride or selfish ambitions (Look at Phil 2:3.). While this quarreling has not yet brought a church split, these witnesses are not supporting unity. They need to stand together against persecution and false teachers. These two women have been good friends and also are good friends of Paul.[2] Their testimony of standing together previously had been a witness their world needed to see. Such a positive testimony today is a witness our world still needs to see.

Read Philippians 1:27-28 and consider the opposites. What happens when we do not stand firm together?

1.
2.
3.
4.
5.

Philippians 1:28. When we stand alone, we can be *afraid* of persecution. If we allow the enemy or other people to intimidate us, we may not make wise decisions. Our decisions should reflect the gospel and the need for the gospel message.

The term for *alarmed* in this verse represents *a startled horse*. We should not be surprised at persecution. We are not to fear as though we have no protection. We have protection from the Lord and from other people in the church community. We have salvation, but opponents of the gospel will face destruction.

What is the sign of destruction for the opponents? (Reread verse 27 for help with the answer.)

---

2   Gordon D. Fee, *God's Empowering Presence: The Holy Spirit in the Letter of Paul* (Peabody, MA: Hendrickson Publishers, 2002), 746.

How does standing firm *with one mind and in one spirit* portray the sign of destruction for the enemies of the gospel?

How does standing firm act as salvation for us?

Describe a time when you were afraid to be a Christian, but encouragement helped make you stronger—buoyed you and emboldened you—to witness or stand firm.

The term for *unafraid*, or *in no way afraid*, means *an un-terrified attitude*. We can have the confidence to stand firm in faith, to work together for the faith, and to see salvation for ourselves and others.

What does this *salvation* in Philippians 1:27-28 mean if we already have a personal relationship with Christ?

According to Philippians 1:27-28, where do we get the strength to stand and fight?

The destruction of the opponents refers to their inability to stand up to the Lord or His people. Our salvation means we have God standing with us and using our suffering for His glory.

Read the following quote from "The Introduction" of *The Embarrassed Believer* by Hugh Hewitt:

> The Embarrassed Believer has already begun to put some distance between Christ's words of Mark 8:38 and Paul's double imperative of 2 Timothy 1:8-9 and himself/herself . . . "nowhere does the church appear less confident than in the United States" . . . there is also a far more pervasive self-censorship and timidity among even the most devoted and authentic Christians . . . The Lord did not counsel a shy and mincing faith but a bold embrace of belief in Him, his Father, and the Holy Spirit.[3]

What do you think of this quote?

If you are a believer in another country, does this quote apply to Christians and churches in your area?   Explain your answer.

---

[3]   Hugh Hewitt, *The Embarrassed Believer: Reviving Christian Witness in an Age of Unbelief* (Nashville: Word Publishing, 1998).

What is necessary for the church to change in the way Paul desires?

Philippians 1:29-30. We may not want to experience what Paul says could happen when we believe in Jesus. We accept the "believe in Him" part. However, Paul says "not only . . . but also."

Read the following passages. Beside each one, tell how we are to handle suffering:

Roman 5:3:
Philippians 1:18:
James 1:2:
1 Peter 1:3-9:

If the world is to find Christ, we are to accept sufferings *joyfully*. We should consider suffering a *gracious gift* from God. We will see later what Paul personally thinks about suffering.

How do you feel about suffering as a gift of grace?

Why do we suffer?

1.
2.

From 1 Peter 1:3-9, list the reasons we can stand firm and can rejoice.

God bestows faith, courage, His indwelling Holy Spirit, the body of believers, oneness with Christ, AND, the privilege to suffer with Jesus. Suffering with Christ reflects our being in oneness with the Lord—with His life and His death. When we accept Jesus as Savior, and therefore Lord, we accept the entire package of being a Christian. The Song of Paul's life includes joy in the suffering—whatever that distress may look like. The proper attitude for our suffering and standing firm appears in Philippians 2.

Philippians 2:1-4. Read the letter below from Amy Wilson. She wrote this while ministering in Vologda, Russia.

Ahh, Learning Lessons, Again

Dear praying friends,

We all have our journey to take. Mine is unique. Yours is unique. Yet each is a journey marked with lessons learned through joy and pain. The way isn't easy, but it is worthwhile. Sometimes we forget that the pain too serves a purpose. Joy is often the result of pain. Indeed it is our ability to feel deep pain that gives us our ability to feel deep joy (or vice versa). Somehow we can't have one without the other. But we often think we'd be happy in the middle. Let us feel neither joy nor pain, but then, what beauty would life hold for us? What motivation? How would we experience the presence of God if we had no capacity to feel deep joy? And no deep joy could be experienced without the ability to also experience deep pain. As for me, I'll take the joy and the pain, if it means I'll experience God's presence, His pleasure, His delight over me.

My time with God today began with prayer. In my prayer time, I sought God's guidance. I remembered how He had walked with me in my life through decisions which led me here. I came here because I felt God was leading here. This is where my heart was. But when I got here, I struggled: what did God bring me here for? What is the point? How will I know if this time is successful or not? The questions have been very much on my mind. But then I felt God speak to these.

The Lord reminded me that I could do all the good in the world and I would still fail. I could try to do things for Him, and I might find myself frustrated. There is only one sure focus for my life which will always lead to success. That is to focus on Him alone. If, in my daily life, I devote myself to knowing Him, communing with Him, then I will be filled. And out of the overflow of His presence in me, the power of God would begin to touch those around me. I may never see "results" but that will not matter since my priority is my communion with God. As I know Him more, His desires will become my desires and His purposes will be accomplished.

I was reminded that the people I admired throughout my life—people like George Mueller, Amy Carmichael, Hudson Taylor—missionaries who all saw God do amazing things. But they witnessed these things not because they sought them, but because they sought God—to know Him for themselves. From their communion with Him, they saw Him do great things.

After my prayer time, I read a devotional from *Voices of the Faithful* (Beth Moore), and the heading was Psalm 37:4. "Delight yourself in the Lord and He will give you the desires of your heart." I also read from the Scriptures 1 John 2:15-17, Revelation 3:1-6, and Isaiah 38.

Revelation says, "You have a reputation of being alive, but you are dead." Outwardly, it's easy to "look" like you have it all together, you are faithful in your walk with God, and people will assume that you are in communion with God. Yet, in truth, you can be far from God and His desires for you.

1 John says, "Do not love the world." I find it easy to fall into the trap of loving the world. While we can enjoy the things of the world—its people, its entertainment, its coffee ;-), we can't love them supremely and live for God, too.

Isaiah 38:17 says, "Surely it was for my benefit that I suffered anguish." I don't believe that we always benefit from pain, but there are times in our lives when God allows this for a purpose. Hezekiah, speaking in Isaiah 38, understood that this was the case in his life at the time. I believe that sometimes it's the case in my life when I go through a difficult time. (Even the culture shock from this week :-)

In *Hinds Feet on High Places*, Much Afraid is again suffering disappointment because she doesn't seem to be heading toward the High Places. She builds another altar and then she's led on by Sorrow and Suffering, her two companions. She comes out of the desert and her breath is taken away by the awakening spring before her. This paragraph struck me:

Much-Afraid told herself that never before had she realized what the awakening from the death of winter was like. Perhaps it had needed the desert wastes to open her eyes to all this beauty, but she walked through the wood, almost forgetting for a little that Sorrow and her sister walked with her....
"...The delay was not unto death but for the glory of God." (HFOHP)

Oh how true these words ring! The winters of our soul serve a purpose, too. The most difficult trial produces some fruit in our lives. The book of James says, "Consider it pure joy, my brothers, whenever you face trials of many kinds, because you know that the working of your faith produces perseverance. Perseverance must finish its work so that you may be mature and complete, not lacking anything." (James 1:2-4)

How easy it is for me to forget that Jesus taught that the way up was to go down. "If any man will come after Me, he must deny himself, take up his cross daily, and follow Me." (Luke 9:23)

This has been a long email. But the winter has been a long one, too. (Figuratively, of course. The real winter hasn't even hit Russia yet.) And there is much to say about the spring, now that my heart is thawing.

Praying that your testimony isn't one of a winter. But if it is, there is a spring ahead. May God bless and keep you.

For His Name and for His Glory.[4]

---

[4] Amy Wilson, "Ah, Learning Lessons, Again" (Vologda: an unpublished email, 2008). Amy served for two years as an ESL teacher in Vologda, Russia, and now serves with a Christian ministry in Texas.

Amy recommends several authors to help us live as we should. I highly recommend Beth Moore's book *Get Out of the Pit: Straight Talk about God's Deliverance.* I tend to be a pit dweller. I am a *lot* better than I used to be, but I can drop into a pit quicker than I should. However, now I know how to look up and let God pull me up with His encouragement. Encouragement is what Paul discusses in Philippians 2:1-4. *If* we have ever been in the pit, and ***because*** we have experienced God's rescuing us through encouragement, we can stop living in the pit of discouragement or despair.

After reading Philippians 2:1-4, list the things which encourage you.

Philippians 2:1-2. The word *if* implies *since* in 2:1. The form of verses 1-2 also is in the form of a conditional: "If . . . , then."

The "if-then" statement is a "first-class conditional," which means the "if" part of the statement is true. That is why we can use the word "since" for "if." The assertions of the "if" phrases in verse 1 promote the expectations or commands in verse 2. Before we study verse 2, we need to discuss verse 1 thoroughly.

Read John 16:7. What name does Jesus call the One to come?

What is the Greek word for this Person who is to come?" (Many pastors have referred to this Greek word in sermons.)

The Greek word for *encouragement* in Philippians 2:1 is the same root as the name *Paraclete*, a term describing the Holy Spirit. You may have heard the word Counselor or Comforter for the person in John 16:7. The word implies *another Jesus*. Just as Jesus encouraged His disciples and told them that another Encourager was coming, Jesus was saying another like Himself would take His earthly place. Actually the meaning of the word *paraclesis* in Philippians 2:1a means more than "encouragement." The literal translation says *the act of embolding another in belief or course of action.*[5] We could say, "Therefore, if in Christ there has been any act of embolding you in your belief or course of action, then . . ."

Read 2 Corinthians 1:3-7. List the number of times a form of the word *comfort* is used.

In Philippians 2:1a, where do we get this encouragement?

---

[5]   *BDAG*, s. v. παραχλέσις.

The word in 2 Corinthians 1:3-7 is the same word for *encouragement* in Philippians 2:1a. This kind of encouragement or comfort comes through our relationship in Christ. The word for the Greek *in*, ἐιν *(ein)*, has many varied meanings, but for Philippians 2:1 the word indicates we have *the marker of position*. We believers are *located in* Christ. That is the *place* we live. We are *in Christ* and because of that position, we receive His act of embolding.

> List ways you have found encouragement in Christ to increase your faith or move you to action.

The word for *consolation* in 2:1b also means *encouragement*. The literal translation of consolation is *that which offers encouragement*.[6] The whole *if … consolation* phrase can mean *if there is any solace offered by love*. Encouragement comes through *alleviating* what troubles us. The solace originates in love.[7] Another way of expressing this thought is that consolation *draws the mind aside from care*. Christ's consolation, because of His love, alleviates fears and hurts by pulling our minds from those concerns.[8]

> How has Christ's love brought you consolation?

> In what ways did the Lord alleviate or draw your mind away from your cares and concerns?

> What Greek word do you think might be used for *fellowship* in 2:1c?

We often hear that true fellowship, *koinonia*, means we have a close relationship with someone. The word can mean we have an attitude of *good will* in *close relationship* with others. In the Bible, koinonia means people are such treasured friends they eat at each other's tables. We have *koinonia* with the Holy Spirit, and the fellowship is very intimate. Therefore, we have the right attitude because God's Spirit is *in communion* with us moment-by-moment,[9] as if we were sitting around a table talking about everything.

This phrase about fellowship can also represent a *partnership with the Spirit*.[10] In other words, we have a connection with God's Spirit so we can partner with Him in God's work. He prepares our hearts with the right attitude towards people.

---

[6] *BDAG*, s. v. παραμύθιον.

[7] Ibid.

[8] Cleon L. Rogers, Jr., and Cleon L. Rogers III, *The New Linguistic and Exegetical Key to the Greek New Testament* (Grand Rapids: ZondervanPublishingHouse, 1998), 451.

[9] *BDAG*, s. v. κοινωνία.

[10] A. T. Robertson, *Word Pictures in the New Testament* (Nashville: Holman Bible Publishers, 2000), under the WordSearch Program.

When have you experienced this kind of *koinonia*?

When do you feel closest to the Spirit?

Have you ever felt you were in partnership with the Spirit?　　　　When?

When have you sensed this kind of fellowship or partnership with other people (Phil 1:5)?

In 2:1d Paul mentions *affection* and *compassion*. Affection comes from the concept of our *inward parts*. If I may be so bold, I would like to put it this way: "If anyone has had *gut feelings* for us." In other words, if anyone ever showed us a merciful heart, if we ever have experienced someone's inner compassion, if another person tangibly has displayed serious concern over our troubles, then we *know* that person genuinely cares about us.[11]

List some times when you received heart-felt affection and compassion from someone other than a family member.

How did you know the affection or compassion was real?

What did you want to do in response to that kind of compassion?

In verse 2:1 Paul establishes the unity people should have with others. Paul wants his readers, including us, to remember the times when the Lord's Spirit and others have cared about our welfare. When we experience the kind of comfort and compassion in verse 1, we should readily respond to Paul's command in verse 2 with a resounding, "Yes! Of course!"

Philippians 2:2. Why would Paul ask his readers to *make his joy complete*?

How could the Philippians, and we, complete Paul's joy?

11　*BDAG*, s. v. οἰκτιρμος and σπλαγχνίζομαι.

Paul was saying, *Fill my cup of joy to its fullest*. We can imagine Paul specifying, "I want to hear of your attitude in a way that brings joy to my heart." Joy can mean *delight*.[12] Paul might be telling his readers, "I want to delight in you and your attitude." The purpose or goal of Paul's joy lies in God's people being of the same mind—the same attitude of harmony—maintaining the same love (2:1), united in the same spirit, intent on the same purpose.

Compare verse 1 with verse 2 in the table below. What part of verse 2 fits each stated part of verse 1?

Verse 1	Verse 2
if there is any encouragement in Christ (by embolding another in belief) **if there is any consolation of love** **if there is any fellowship of the Spirit** **if any affection and compassion**	

An interesting development in the Greek of verse 2 is called an *inclusio*. An inclusio means the beginning and ending of the passage are the same or similar. In verse 2, the word for *of the same mind* and *intent on the same purpose* is the same Greek word. Paul begins and ends the verse with the same word as if those phrases were brackets for the other words.[13]

Paul knows that for Christ's work to go forward, God's people must think the same kinds of thoughts. We must live in harmony in our thinking.[14] In other words, Paul demands we live and act in unity of purpose.

In comparing 2:1 with 2:2, we can combine the first part of verse 2 with the first part of verse 1, and the last part of verse 2 with the last part of verse 1. The middle parts should align as well. We might even read the verses as:

2:1 If there is any encouragement in Christ . . . 2:2 make my joy complete by being of the same mind,

2:1 If there is any consolation of love . . . 2:2 make my joy complete by maintaining the same love,

2:1 If there is any fellowship with the Spirit . . . 2:2 make my joy complete by being united in spirit,

2:1 If there is any affection and compassion . . . 2:2 make my joy complete by being intent on one purpose.

Paul does not divide the verses this way, however. All the parts of verses 1 and 2 combine to remind us why we should maintain a Christ-like attitude, fellowship with the Spirit, and unity in the church. Paul knows the church has to be intent on the same purpose to survive.

---

[12] Richard R. Melick, Jr., *Philippians, Colossians, Philemon*, NAC 32 (Nashville: Broadman Press, 1991), 30.

[13] The Greek words are φρονέω, φρονέο. We get the English words, *phrenic* or *frenetic*, meaning *frenzied* or *frantic* from φρονέω. All these issues describe the mind.

[14] *BDAG*, s. v. φρονέω.

How would Paul expect us to be of one mind, intent on the same purpose?

All four words in verse one are synonyms for encouragement. Let's interpret the verses another way and use "since" instead of "if":

2:1 Since there is encouragement *in Christ* . . . 2:2 make my joy complete by being of the same mind,

2:1 Since there is encouragement *of love* . . . 2:2 make my joy complete by maintaining the same love,

2:1 Since there is encouragement *with the Spirit* . . . 2:2 make my joy complete by being united in spirit,

2:1 Since there is encouragement *through compassion* . . . 2:2 make my joy complete by being intent on one purpose.

In order to make Paul's joy complete with the attitude that Christ wants, we must recognize we have no excuses not to be in agreement with other believers. The encouragement, encouragement, encouragement, and encouragement of verse 1 insist we live in unity with a loving spirit. Unity does not mean sameness. All the phrases align from the reassurance of Christ, His Spirit, and His people. We find the way to unity in 2:3.

Philippians 2:3. Paul restates verses 1-2 another way.

To a Hebrew like Paul, in order to emphasize his point, he might use parallelism either positively or negatively. He uses *antithetical parallelism* in this verse and also in verse 4 to instruct his readers first negatively and then positively. His readers are to do nothing that would not fulfill his joy. *Nothing* emphatically means *no thing, in no way do anything*. We are to do nothing selfishly or from vain conceit.[15]

Selfish ambition (NIV), *selfishness* (NASU), or *strife* (KJV) comes from the root word meaning *day laborer*. This word illustrates *rivalry* or *wrong determination* in the workplace. People might push to have a place of honor at work, make better wages, or receive a promotion before someone else. The attitude relates to a *self-seeking outlook*.[16]

Vainglory (KJV) or *empty conceit* (NIV) refers to desiring glory, honor, praise, or worship.[17] Paul is very aware of OT Scriptures which teach how God protects His glory. Paul knows the danger of seeking what belongs to God.

---

[15] Sharon L. Gresham, "Philippians," An Unpublished Paper for Dr. William B. Tolar, *Hermeneutics* (Fort Worth: SWBTS, 2003)

[16] Ralph P. Martin, *The Epistle of Paul to the Philippians* (Grand Rapids: William B. Eerdmans Publishing Company, 1988), 96.

[17] *Strong's Greek and Hebrew Dictionary*, s. v. vainglory (2754), under *Free Bible Tools*, http://www.blueletterbible.org/lang/lexicon/lexicon.cfm?Strongs=G2745&t=KJV (accessed February 1, 2012).

Read the following passages. Write what God does and why:

Exodus 33:18-22:

Isaiah 42:8:

1 Corinthians 1:31:

God does not completely show or yield His full glory to anyone. Therefore, we are not to boast about ourselves, anyone else, or anything except God. Any other boasting would be *empty conceit* (NASU). We certainly can be pleased with what we achieve, but we must handle our accomplishments appropriately. We can give the Lord the glory for what He has allowed us to do.

Paul prefers *humility* to self-importance or conceit. The KJV translates the Greek word for humility: *lowliness of mind*. The implication is that people humble themselves, or place themselves at a lower point.[18]

In Asia, when people meet someone they think is better or older than they, they bow lower than the other person. Even on campus at the seminary I attended for my Masters degree, some Asian students would bow lower than I. Possibly it is because they knew my husband and I were missionaries in an Asian country or they thought I was old enough to be a professor. I was just a much older student.

Placing ourselves lower than others shows we regard them as persons of greater value. The term *regard* means *to esteem others as we would a governor or ruler*. The word for *more important* (2:3) combines two Greek words *huper* or *hyper—to hold above*, and *echo—to maintain*. In this verse, Paul says that we should hold others above ourselves and keep them there as if they rule over us. Therefore, we esteem them by lowering or humbling ourselves.

Read 1 Peter 5:6. What preposition does Peter use about *where* we are to humble ourselves?

The word for *under* is *hupo* or *hypo*. That word gives us the idea for "hypodermic." A hypodermic needle goes under the skin. The word "hypochondriac" means *under the influence of imaginary ailments*. In 1 Peter 5:6, the Greek *hypo* implies *under the control of*. We are to humble ourselves *under the control of* God. The verse gives a good reason why we should humble ourselves. This word is in direct contrast to how we are to treat others.

Read the last part of 1 Peter 5:6 again. Why does God want our humility?

---

[18]   *BDAG*, s. v. ταπειοφροσύνη.

God wants to lift us *up*. The Greek word implies He may exalt us in honor, power, or position. While we are still *under* His control, He lifts us *up*. He lifts us higher than we can ever place ourselves or our endeavors.[19]

Once in advising a friend, via email, about the disgrace a fellow believer was experiencing, I remembered a message our pastor Rob Zinn had preached in San Bernardino, California, in the late 1970's. He spoke on Nebuchadnezzar from Daniel 4:28-37. In teaching on that king's fall, Rob said God will warn us about our pride privately. If we do not repent, the Lord will warn us publicly. If we still do not repent, He may disgrace us publicly (Daniel 4).[20]

As I spelled the word *disgrace* in the email, the word jumped from the page in two fragments: dis grace. First Peter 5:6 immediately came to mind. God desires to *grace* us. Grace is what He prefers to do, but He will allow *dis*-grace if necessary. In order to keep from dis-grace, we need to humble ourselves under God and lift others up.

Read 1 Peter 5:5. List what we are to do and why:

1.
2.

God opposes the proud. He dis-graces them.

Has God spoken to you privately about a matter in your life that needs changing? When?

Did He have to go to a public warning?   When?

Allow a public disgrace?   When?

Instead of allowing God to *grace* you by lifting you up, in what other areas of your life could you cause Him to *dis-grace* you?

Talk about a holy elevation! God *lifts* us if we *lower* us. What a way to receive honor!

First Peter 5:6 tells us we humble ourselves under what?

Humbling ourselves under the control of the mighty or *strong hand* of God, we place ourselves in the safest, most elevated place we can. In reality when we place ourselves under God's

19   *BDAG*, s. v. ὑψόω.
20   Used by permission of Rob Zinn (January 25, 2012). Zinn stated that he was preaching from a series which Charles Stanley wrote on Daniel. Rob preached at Emmanuel Baptist Church, San Bernardino, CA (1978).

mighty hand, we are *in* His hand—that position of being in Christ. Remember what Paul says in Philippians 2:3, "Put yourself under others, and esteem them over you, maintaining them there as a ruler over you."[21] We can do that by putting ourselves under God's hand.

Read Mark 12:28-31. How does Mark correspond with Philippians 2:1-2?

What encouragement do you find in these Markan verses?

Philippians 2:4. Paul gives us further insight in how to accomplish 2:1-3. He continues the idea of humility. We *look to the interests* of others.

NOTE: even when we look to the interests of others, we must look to our interests, too. We must love ourselves. Paul does not say we do not look after our needs at all.

Look, skopeo, is the word from which we get *scope. Skopeo* can be translated *scope it out, carefully consider things, notice.* Paul intends this scoping to be an ongoing action. We are to consider others' needs as a *goal* of our lives.[22]

Paul uses the same Greek word in Philippians 3:14 when he discusses "pressing toward the *goal* to win a prize." Our *goal* or *scope* is setting others above ourselves, fixing our eyes on the needs of others, and seeking the good of others to promote the unity that Paul and the Lord desire.

When we focus on the interests of others, we need to consider our motivations. Think of someone, or several people, with whom you involve yourself. Consider *why* you stay involved with that person, group, or even stay busy with an activity.

Answer the following questions and explain your answers:

Do I want to keep control over that person?

Do I want my opinion to rule more than God's?

Am I willing to let go and let the person fail, if that is what it takes for God to get through to that one?

Do I want praise for helping?

---

[21] We will deal with what to do with harsh "rulers" later. At this point, the emphasis is on how we view others.

[22] *BDAG,* s. v. σκοπέω.

Do I want to be involved because I am nosy?

Am I afraid to let go of helping, because that person might find someone else to help?

Do I find my value in helping rather than placing myself under God?

Do I hang onto that person because I cannot trust God to encourage, console, fellowship, or bring *me* compassion?

Am I a codependent personality who will hang onto the needs of others at the expense of my own dysfunction?

Do I engage in activities so other people will see me and value me for what I do?

We can *selfishly* scope out the needs of others because we are looking out for our own personal interests. We must humbly ask ourselves why we do what we do. Unity demands proper motivation.

Philippians 2:5. While verse 5 starts a new paragraph, and introduces the song in verses 6-11, it continues to emphasize the right mindset we are to have.

Verse 5 is a hinge verse. It ties verses 1:27 with 2:6-11. Verse 5 connects specifically with verse 2a and 2d through the same verb *phroneo* for mind and intent. The bridge verse also links Philippians 1:27-3:21 with the concept of *imitating Christ* in humility and unity.[23]

The Greeks took a dim view of humility. The word for humility was not used with much approval in Greek literature before the New Testament writers included it.[24] Non-Christians equated the term with cowardice.[25]

Christ has given us a different attitude about the word. He has made humility the mark of noblest character.[26] *Attitude* means *adopt a view*. Paul expects believers to adopt Christ's view about humility in spite of what any culture might indicate.

---

[23] Thomas R. Schreiner, *Paul, Apostle of God's Glory in Christ: A Pauline Theology* (Downers Grove, IL: InterVarsity Press, 2001), 169-70.

[24] Archibald M. Hunter, *The Letter of Paul to the Philippians*, LBC, ed. Balmer H. Kelly (Richmond: John Knox Press, 1959), 92.

[25] William Hendriksen, *Exposition of Philippians*, New Testament Commentary 6 (Grand Rapids: Baker Book House, 1962), 100.

[26] Hunter, *The Letter of Paul to the Philippians*, 92.

Read Matthew 20:25-28. What does Jesus expect of His followers?

How does the Lord expect us to exercise authority?

The Lord of lords said in order to be great in His Kingdom, we must serve and give our lives. Paul indicates that we believers continually should cherish and exhibit Christ's servanthood as we work together. Our attitude should be like Christ's because that is how we handle problems.[27] Beth Moore in *Get Out of that Pit* states that "*together* is the whole point of any process."[28] In order to work together with God, our outlook must be like Christ's. I think Jan Moses has it:

Sunday, January 14, 2007 8:46 PM CST

Jan is about the same. She still is breathing on her own through the tracheotomy. She occasionally has bouts of painful coughing followed by shallow breathing. Today, with lots of effort, she swallowed a little water. Her blood pressure and heart rate are still OK. No fever. Her coordination seems a bit improved. It is still too early to assess her speech abilities. Tomorrow morning they will place a ventricular shunt from her head just behind her ear, channel it beneath her skin, and have it drain into her abdomen. The doctor is still optimistic that she should be ready to fly (literally) to Texas by Wednesday.

Well, I think I may know one reason why God allowed Jan to be in that bed instead of me. I would have wimped out. I would rather enjoy heaven than to endure this level of pain. I would have never called 911. "Lord, take me now! Let's get this over with." And if I did make the mistake of calling 911, I wouldn't have told them where my medical records were. The less they know, the quicker I'll go. Gosh, I probably wouldn't have bothered to keep medical records.

But, unlike me, Jan is not thinking about "I", but about you, and about her Lord. I think she wants to preserve every opportunity she has to make Christ known, even at the cost of terrible suffering. I suspect that the power of our testimony is not in the crafting of eloquent words, but in the simple, bold statements of faith spoken in the backdrop of adverse circumstances. In the past days, Jan has given us thumbs up affirmations of her dependence and trust in the Lord, Jesus Christ. And this in the midst of unspeakable pain, both physical and emotional.

Still, I don't want to presume on anything. Satan's goal is to use suffering as a wedge to separate us from God. God's goal is to use the same suffering as a means to purify our faith and lead us into a deeper fellowship with Him. While most of us can well endure

---

[27]   Hendriksen, *Exposition of Philippians*, 102.
[28]   Beth Moore, *Get Out of That Pit: Straight Talk about God's Deliverance from a Former Pit Dweller* (Nashville: Integrity Publishers, 2007), 145.

a moment of suffering, there's something about persistent, unrelenting pain that surely tears at the fabric of our faith and challenges the sturdiest of souls.

So, in the ICU room, I see a bigger battle going on than just the physical recovery of Jan's mind and body. I see a struggle in her soul. When I came into her room this afternoon, she grabbed my hand and, with panic in her eyes, mouthed words that were not about her physical condition, but about some emotional fears. Pray for Jan's spirit; that the arrows of the enemy will not find their mark. Pray that she will once again be able to verbally make Christ known.[29]

Let's each consider our attitudes. I am more like Mark, I think. When I am sick or as is often my case—on medication that brings depression—I wonder if I am more concerned about the physical condition or that I cannot "verbally make Christ known."

How about you?

The Christ Hymn: Glorifying and Imitating the Lord (2:6-11)

Philippians 2:6-11. The New International Version (NIV) writes this passage in poem form. Most commentators believe these six verses comprise one of the earliest Christian hymns, perhaps sung by believers in Antioch.

While Paul may have written the hymn himself, he may have learned it in Antioch from the church that encouraged him in his early ministry. Wherever he may have gotten it, he weaves its poetic elements into his letter. One scholar believes the song echoes throughout the letter. Paul seems to reinforce literary and vocabulary parallels from the song throughout the body of the letter (1:3-4:20). Whatever the source, Paul certainly liked to sing or even say hymns and doxologies—as we have already mentioned and as we have seen in his life and letters.[30]

By the time of the letter, Philippians 2:6-11 may have become a creed, but its characteristics of rhythm, rare words, phrases, motifs, and poetic form look like a "hymn" in two stanzas: verses 6-8 and 9-11. The hymn embraces theology, confession, liturgy, arguments, and doxology.[31] The depth of theology relates the powerful image of Jesus as God and man.[32]

The hymn may have been composed originally by a Jewish Christian for the celebration of the Lord's Supper in Palestine.[33] Since the church began in Judaism and continued worshipping in the same way as they had in the synagogues, the song would sound like a Jewish hymn.[34]

---

[29] Mark Moses, an unpublished email; Moses, *An Uncommon Faith*, 187-88. Used by Permission from Mark Moses. Jan had been able to travel to family in another state, but had to enter a hospital there for a few days.

[30] Acts 16; Gorman, *Apostle of the Crucified Lord*, 418-50.

[31] Peter O'Brien, *The Epistle to the Philippians: A Commentary on the Greek Text*, NIGTC, ed. I. Howard Marshall and W. Ward Gasque (Grand Rapids: William B. Eerdmans Publishing, 1991), 188.

[32] Melick, *Philippians, Colossians, Philemon*, 97; O'Brien, *The Epistle to the Philippians*, 192.

[33] Ralph P. Martin, *Worship in the Early Church* (Grand Rapids: William B. Eerdmans Publishing Company, 1998), 111.

[34] Ibid., 40.

However, the hymn writer wanted to give Jesus the worship He deserved. Paul incorporates this song to teach the right attitude for life.

Pastor Al Meredith at Wedgwood Baptist Church in Fort Worth, Texas, will break into a hymn or praise chorus as it fits within his sermon. The congregation usually joins him. When they are finished with the song, he proceeds with his message.[35] Surely Paul praised his Lord Jesus Christ when he preached, since we see doxologies and hymns in his written messages.

In Ephesians 3:20-21, Paul breaks into doxology after his prayer message that his readers understand the love of Christ. "Paul closed his prayer with a doxology. He praised God **who is able to do far more than** one could **ask or imagine, according to** the standard of **His power**."[36] Harold Hoehner entitles this section of Ephesians, "The Ascription of Praise."[37] How true of Paul to give praise to the Lord in every circumstance, and to believe that God's power is His normal way of working in, through, and for us.

Philippians 2:6. The hymn verses portray Jesus Christ as the One whose mindset believers should follow.

In 2:6, Paul introduces Christ as being in the form of God first. Literally, the Greek says, *Who in the form of God existing. Existing* is *to be at hand, starting, or ruling. Form* usually indicates *shape*. The actual shape, or the idea of "being *equally* (something) to God",[38] is not known. The expression indicates Jesus is *exactly God*.

Read John 4:24-26. What form do you see in these verses?

What we see in the *form* is *exact equality*. Even as "the Son," Christ was and is fully divine, as fully God as the Father in every way: being, character, image, etc. *Equality* indicates *sameness* or *consistency*.

Read Colossians 1:15-20. Compare the two hymns:

Philippians 2:6-11   **Colossians 1:15-20**

---

[35] I personally encountered this practice and enjoyed worship in this way at Wedgwood Baptist Church: Al Meredith, pastor, Wedgwood Baptist Church, Fort Worth, TX. Used by permission from Wedgwood Baptist Church.

[36] Harold W. Hoehner, "Ephesians," in *Bible Knowledge Commentary: New Testament*, ed. John F. Walvoord, and Roy B. Zuck (Wheaton: Scripture Press, 1983; now under David C. Cook), 632. Publisher permission required to reproduce. All rights reserved.

[37] Ibid.

[38] Ben Witherington III, *Jesus the Sage: The Pilgrimage of Wisdom* (Minneapolis: Fortress Press, 1994), 262.

What differences do you see?

What do you learn about Jesus in both of these passages?

What helps you concerning the meaning of *image* or *form*?

What questions do you have concerning either passage?

Now read Galatians 4:19 and Hebrews 1:2-4. What similarities do you see in these passages with Philippians 2:6-11 and Colossians 1:15-20?

What more do the two hymns tell you about Jesus?

What OT prophecies do the hymns represent?

In Philippians 2:6, *did not regard*, or *consider* (NIV), repeats the word Paul used for *consider* each person better than yourself in 2:3. Christ did not regard His position as God too important to humble Himself. His oneness with the Father was not something that Christ could lose even if He lowered Himself.

Grasped relays something *seized* or *clutched as in robbery*. The **pre-incarnate**, **pre-existing** Son of God already possessed equality with the Father, so He could not rob God of equality. Christ resolved not to cling to the equal position with a firm grip, but give Himself for humanity. What we can see is the contrast of someone who wants to be self-centered and seek his or her own good rather than help others. God's nature is to give. Christ demonstrated giving rather than clasping.

At this point I am about to go deep. I will bring two different interpretations into the study of the hymn. You may have heard the first explanation most of your life in sermons on Philippians 2:6-11.

Some people draw the parallel between the "first and last Adam." They compare Adam and Jesus. Paul introduced the comparison of Adam and Christ in 1 Corinthians 15:45-48. Recently, some scholars have disagreed with the Adam/Christ comparison as an explanation for Philippians 2:6. Since their reasons and my explanation may get pretty involved, please hang in there with me. I will try to use the first example as an illustration of how we should live when things get tough in our lives or when we endure temptation—that is what I think Paul may have been doing *even if* he did not refer to what Adam/Eve did wrong.

Other theologians do not agree that Philippians 2:6-8 echo or allude to Genesis 3.[39] We will look at their reasons more fully later, but introduce three reasons here:

First, some of the Adam/Christ scholars try to explain the hymn just with Jesus' humanity. They do not think the hymn's theology teaches the pre-existence of Christ. I cannot do that. The concept of Christ lowering Himself has to mean Paul implies the pre-existence. Christ had to be equal to God before He could grasp any equality or lower Himself.

Second, the scholars say no *explicit* Adam/Christ language exists in the hymn. Paul does not use the terms "Adam," or "the Fall" that might immediately cause readers to consider the comparison of Adam and Jesus. However, Paul is comparing Christ to something, or someone, that grasps what it should not have.

Third, the scholars indicate Paul uses a different Greek word for *form* in Philippians than in 1 Corinthians, so he was trying to *avoid* an Adam/Christ analogy. However, in Galatians Paul uses that same Greek word in his Adam-Christ comparison with the idea that Jesus Christ restores the image Adam ruined.

While I firmly agree with the idea that we have to accept Christ's preexistence, I do not entirely agree that no allusion/echo to Genesis 3 exists. One word could cause first-century readers to remember something Paul taught or even to think about a Bible story. In that case, not grasping equality possibly could have reminded the readers how Adam and Eve desired equality with God.

A lot of Paul's teachings echo the OT and Creation. Those themes were fully engrained in his thought. Since Paul uses the Adam/Christ comparison in 1-2 Corinthians, and says Jesus *restores the form or image* of Christ in Galatians, we can see a possible echo of comparison with Adam/Eve to Jesus. Paul uses synonyms for *form*, *likeness*, and *image* throughout his letters. In Philippians 2:6 Paul uses the noun in Galatians 4:19 (*morphe*, μορφή) from the same Greek verb where we get *to morph* or *change*.

Therefore, I choose to pursue the comparison of Adam/Eve to Christ. I think we can learn a very important lesson in how we are to handle circumstances in our lives. Some may consider my idea "devotionalizing," or trying to make a passage say something it doesn't really say. Since a lot of scholars and pastors have interpreted the passage in the first way, I want to include that comparison for the hymn. We do need to consider the second way of investigating the meaning of the hymn and will do so after looking at the possible Adam/Christ analogy.

I would like us to compare the difference in Adam/Eve and Jesus in their attitudes towards temptations. We may be tempted to take God's place in our trials. The Philippians had to face similar struggles in their circumstances. Paul wanted them to see how Jesus handled His.

In order to proceed in the first discussion, I would like us to consider the following passages. Each one uses μορφή for *form*, *likeness*, or *image*. Notice how each passage uses the word.

Read the following passages and tell how the authors use the word for form:

---

[39] Gordon D. Fee, *Pauline Christology: An Exegetical-Theological Study* (Peabody, MA: Hendrickson Publishers, 2007), 376-93. These pages are Fee's explanation of his disagreement. I give the full reference of page numbers so readers may go his book and study for themselves; Peter Thomas O'Brien, *The Epistle to the Philippians*, NIGTC, s. v. Philippians 2:6, 7, 8.

Job 4:16:

Isaiah 44:13:

Daniel 4:33:

Galatians 4:19:

Daniel and several passages from the LXX use the *same word* for form of God *and* man. In Galatians 4:19, Paul indicates that Christ continues to be *formed* in each believer. His image is in us, but He wants to make that image very clear like God originally intended. Therefore Christ continues to work in our lives. Let's consider image and equality in Philippians 2:6.

Comparison of Adam/Eve and Christ

From the background of the Genesis story, the devil as tempter persuaded Eve and Adam that they could become like God, equal with Him in knowledge and wisdom. Adam and Eve coveted God's ability, as if they should be in the same place—with the same status.

Christ did not need to clutch divine equality in those areas. The Lord already possessed them. Christ did not have to covet remaining in His own place. He could not gain what He already had. Instead, He was willing to put Himself in the form of humanity so He could re-mold people in the form of God.[40]

Within our lives, we often act like Adam and Eve. We may not think we try to become equal with God. However, when we hang onto something God tells us to let go, we tell God we know what we should do as well as He does.

Read Genesis 3:1-6, Matthew 4:1-11, and 1 John 2:15-16. Notice how the enemy tempts us. There are three basic categories of temptation. In the table below we begin with 1 John 2:15-16. John has made it easy for us by giving us the three categories. We can match what happened in the Garden of Eden with what Jesus endured in the wilderness. In the table, match the categories with the other two Scriptures.

Types of Temptations

1 JOHN 2:16	GENESIS 3:6	MATTHEW 4:1-11

---

40   Martin, *Worship in the Early Church*, 101-102; Thomas R. Schreiner, *Paul: Apostle of God's Glory in Christ*, 105, 106; Witherington, *Jesus the Sage*, 264; Fee, *Pauline Christology*, 383.

Contrast Eve's response with Jesus'. What made the difference for the Lord in response to temptation?

Reread Genesis 3:5 and Matthew 4:10. In the table express how Eve and Jesus handled being like God within each of their temptations.

Eve	Jesus
1.	1.
2.	2.
3.	3.

We have examples of what to do and what not to do during temptation. Although Jesus is God, on His earthly pilgrimage He still had to endure temptation concerning His divinity. He had to decide whether to use His divinity inappropriately—to grasp it in an ungodly way. Satan wanted the Lord's power and wanted Jesus to grasp onto His power in the same way Adam and Eve wanted it.

Jesus handled His divinity correctly. He knew the Word of God clearly, quoted it appropriately, and responded correctly when He was tempted. Eve—and Adam—did not.

The word for *grasping* in the Greek means Adam and Eve wanted to clench onto the likeness of God. Was that entirely wrong?

Read Genesis 1:26-27. What did they already have?

Why do you think Adam and Eve might have wanted to grasp onto *equality* with God?

Adam and Eve thought they knew better than God what was good for them. They thought God was withholding good things from them. They also did not trust God to care for them adequately.

Let's look at another aspect of Jesus' handling temptation. We see both the ideas of temptation and trials in Luke 22:39-46. Read the passage. How did Jesus handle the temptation of His trial?

Read 1 Corinthians 10:12-13. How are we to handle temptation?

How can we trust that God will keep us from succumbing to temptation even when trials are hard?

Jesus trusted the Father to take care of Him. As God, He could have decided to take things into His own hands. He deserved worship. However, as man He had to trust the Father and follow God's plan. Adam and Eve rivaled God by trusting, and therefore worshipping, themselves and the snake. They trusted God's creatures rather than God the Creator. Such thinking demonstrates the error of their reasoning. They did not see that succumbing to temptation placed them under the source of temptation, rather than under God's protective hand.[41]

Philippians 2:6 continues what 2:4 implies. In reasoning that we can grasp onto equality with God, we like Adam and Eve begin to grasp created things around us. A. W. Tozer in *The Pursuit of God* deals with the *tyranny of things*. The things God created are gifts to us, just as the tree of the knowledge of good and evil was in the Garden of Eden. Too often we have taken things and put them on the throne of our hearts.[42]

We also do that with people. Such acts are idolatry. Grasping involves coveting God's place and the things He gives. Coveting links with idolatry.

Reread Isaiah 44:13. To what form does this passage refer?

To have the same mind as Christ, we must take each thing, person, and position, and give each one back to God for His control.[43]

Read Genesis 22. To *whom* are you grasping?

Read Exodus 4. To *what* are you grasping?

Read Luke 9:23-26. To *what in yourself* are you grasping?

---

[41] Schreiner, *Paul: Apostle of God's Glory in Christ*, 105.

[42] A. W. Tozer, *The Pursuit of God: The Human Thirst for the Divine* (Camp Hill, PA: WingSpread Publishers, 1993), 21-29.

[43] Schreiner, *Paul: Apostle of God's Glory in Christ*, 105-106; Ben Witherington III, *The Paul Quest: The Renewed Quest for the Jew of Tarsus* (Downers Grove, IL: InterVarsity Press, 1998), 246. Witherington does not believe the hymn contrasts Adam and Christ since Paul would not expect people to worship the Adamic figure. However, people can grasp onto being like God and put devotion for things in the wrong place. In addition, Adam and Eve grasped and therefore sinned. Christ did not grasp His status, but came to earth.

In other words, what things, people, or issues in your life is God asking you to relinquish?

Nothing can be in God's way if we are to be the people He desires. We cannot be who *we* desire to be if we continue to cling to whatever gets in the way of our relationship with the Lord.

Reread Exodus 4:1-5. Then read 14:15-23. What did Moses throw down?

What did God do with what Moses relinquished?

In Genesis 22, what did God command Abraham to "throw down," or put on the altar?

What did God do with what Abraham relinquished?

What might God do with those things you relinquish?

For Moses, the staff was a special tool of the shepherd. Moses had used that stick to defend himself and his sheep. God took Moses' staff and used it to perform miracles for the people of Israel. The staff became God's rod. For Abraham, Isaac was the son for whom Abraham had waited a long time. God used Isaac as Abraham's son of promise through whom the Messiah came.

Some theologians consider Isaac as a *type* of Christ. A *type* means someone in history whose life or actions point to something later.[44] The picture is vivid in this story. Abraham willingly put down his son on the altar of sacrifice; God did as well. God the Father gave His Son on the cross as the sacrifice for sin. Although some other scholars see the ram as the *type* in the Genesis story, both symbols point to the reality that God gave His Son as the sacrifice just as He asked of Abraham.

As in Moses' and Abraham's lives, God wants control of things and people in ours. We cannot grip those things or people too tightly. If they replace Jesus as Lord, He cannot use them. If we grasp those things or people selfishly, we do not let the Lord use us as He would like.

God is not against things or people being special to us. He gives them as gifts for us to enjoy and for us to share with others. When we clutch too tightly, we consider those items ours rather than God's. They can become what possess us rather than God.[45]

Stop and pray with Tozer:

---

44 Wick Broomall, "Type, Typology," in *Baker's Dictionary of Theology*, ed. Everett F. Harrison (Grand Rapids: Baker Book House, 1979), 533-534.

45 Calvin Miller, *Into the Depths of God: Where Eyes See the Invisible, Ears Hear the Inaudible, and Minds Conceive the Inconceivable* (Minneapolis: Bethany House Publishers, 2000), 37-38.

O God and Father, I repent of my sinful preoccupation
with visible things. The world has been too much with me.
Thou hast been here and I knew it not. I have been blind to Thy presence.
Open my eyes that I may behold Thee in and around me.
For Christ's sake ... Amen.[46]

Philippians 2:7. Christ owns everything. He has experienced all of heaven's glory for all of eternity. Nothing has been denied Him. He is God. Still, in His incarnation, Christ chose not to grasp His position with a closed fist, but let go and lower himself to the form of a servant.

Instead of grasping, Christ emptied Himself in two ways:

1. by *adding* humanity;
2. by *setting aside* His Shekinah glory and divine rights.

He chose to make Himself nothing in relation to the status He already had. Christ Jesus modeled total humility and total humanity. He set aside the privileges and attributes of divinity, but they were always present in Him. In so doing, the Lord lowered Himself to the form or characteristic of a *bond-servant*.[47] In other words, Jesus chose to impale Himself like the servant in Exodus (Ex 21).

Where did Jesus allow Himself to be impaled?

The Majestic Son of Glory humbled Himself to die on the cross for our sins.

Questions may arise about just what Christ laid aside when He humbled Himself. The Lord did not lose His full deity of *existence*, *form*, and *equality* with God. *Form of a bond-servant* refers to Jesus' human nature.[48] Christ became 100% human, but remained 100% divine.[49] Jesus Christ possessed both natures in such way that by adding humanity, He maintained His divinity. He is the God-Man in one Personhood.

Read Exodus 24:12-18. Tell why the glory was too hard for people to see.

On earth Jesus divested Himself of position, prestige, and privileges. He shrouded the Shekinah glory—the appearance of deity—which people could not have endured.[50] He chose

---

46   Tozer, *The Pursuit of God*, 67.

47   Schreiner, *Paul, Apostle of God's Glory in Christ*, 170; Witherington, *The Paul Quest*, 247; Witherington, *Jesus the Sage*, 262-64.

48   R. C. H. Lenski, *The Interpretation of St. Paul's Epistles to the Galatians, to the Ephesians, and to the Philippians* (Minneapolis: Augsburg Publishing House, 1961), 781.

49   Hendriksen, *Exposition of Philippians*, 104.

50   *BDAG*, s. v. κενόω.

to cover His majesty. Christ chose to become like us to show us how we could become like Him, to keep us from grasping inappropriately onto God's glory.

> Read Colossians 3:10 and Hebrews 1:3. If we are made in Christ's image, and Christ is exactly God's image, what does that mean?

This does not mean we become *godlings*. We are in God's image and likeness, but we do not become gods, even though He has made us His new creation. God, however, still expects us to live and look like Christ.

> Read 2 Corinthians 1:20; 3:4-18. What does "glory to glory" mean?

> What have you learned about God's glory that Adam and Eve and the people of Israel did not realize?

The lesson not to grasp onto God's glory is the truth Adam and Eve did not understand. They did not realize that God would share His glory. However, God does not give His glory to those who grasp for it. He does not give His place as Almighty God. He lets us participate in His glory as He shines it through us.

The people of Israel did not realize they could share in God's glory the same way Moses did. They did not experience the Shekinah glory because of fear and unbelief. We also do not handle the image, mindset, or glory of God correctly. An improper view of God's glory causes an improper view of ourselves. The right perspective involves the humility we have already discussed.

Philippians 2:8. Christ came to look like us. Jesus Christ could be found in the *fashion, figure,* or *shape* of a human being.

Becoming a man would be a sufficient humbling, but Jesus went further. He *brought* Himself *low* enough to die on a cross. He bowed Himself to allow soldiers to use a nail like an awl on His wrists and feet. Verse 8 indicates the death on the cross was an act of *obedience*, becoming *attentive* to God's will.

> Read Hebrews 5:8. What does the verse say Jesus learned?

> Why would Jesus need to learn obedience?

We need to see two issues in Hebrews 5:8:

First, "even though He were *a* Son" (Heb 5:8) does not mean God had other God-sons and Jesus was one among many. The term implies "as a son." We are called "children of God" but that does not apply here.

Second, the Son of God came to earth to experience what we do. The Son *was educated* in what we experience and what we feel as we suffer. As the perfect One, He would die in *empathy* with His creation. The obedience Jesus learned came through the trials and temptations He suffered as a man. God did not spare Jesus suffering just because He was God.

Through suffering in His earthly life, Jesus could understand and demonstrate how to be obedient to God in our sufferings. Jesus depended on the Holy Spirit for daily living. His obedience would provide the example for our dependence on the Spirit.[51] *Things suffered* can mean *enduring suffering*.[52] Christ experienced just what we would in suffering, but He endured without sin.[53]

Christ's suffering took Him all the way to *death* on a cross. The cross was the instrument of Roman torture and shame. Christ came to understand experientially the temptations, suffering, and emotions in hard times. However, He also came to die for the sin nature that Adam introduced through his disobedience and sins that each person does in yielding to temptation.

Knowing that He purposely bound Himself to servanthood for us, how does that change your perspective on being in fellowship with His suffering?

Philippians 2:9. Reread 1 Peter 5:6.

We can develop an interesting word play in the Greek between these two verses. Paul and Peter do not develop this idea, but I would like us to consider the thought. In 1 Peter 5:6, the Greek word for lifting up is from *hupsao*, ὑψόω. The word for what God does for Jesus in Philippians 2:9 is from *hyperupsao*, ὑπερυψόω.

This exercise in Greek may be getting a bit technical, but notice the prefix on the word for what God does for Jesus. What does the prefix "hyper" mean?

Because of what Jesus did in humbling Himself to the lowest place and offering Himself on the cross, God *exalted* Him. When we humble ourselves, God exalts us. The Father, however, lifted the Son to the *highest—hyper—*place of honor. God exalted Jesus *above and beyond* what God does for us.

The hymn writer uses two interesting rhetorical devices to show Christ's humiliation and exaltation. One figure of speech called a *catabasis*, or gradual descent, shows the Lord's humiliation. The other figure, an *anabasis* or gradual ascent, shows the Lord's glorification.

---

[51] F. F. Bruce, *The Epistle to the Hebrews* (Grand Rapids: Wm. B. Eerdmans Publishing Company, 1979), 102-103.

[52] *NASB Greek & Hebrew Dictionary*, 3958.

[53] *Strong's*, 3958.

Read Philippians 2:6-11. Under the headings write the parts of each stanza (The second column will need some repetition of terms.):

Philippians 2:6-8	Philippians 2:9-11
1.	1.
2.	2.
3.	3.
4.	4.
5.	5.
6.	6.
7.	7.

Notice the first stanza descends seven steps *downward* from being in the form of God to death of the cross. The second stanza ascends seven steps *upward* to glorification.[54]

Based on these scriptures, why can you trust that if you humble yourself, God will exalt you?

Just how do you want God to exalt you?

On earth, Jesus humbled himself *under* God's hand and trusted in the way the Father would exalt Him. Both the death and resurrection were part of the way God elevated Jesus. Jesus was lifted on the cross, even though that seemed a dis-grace, so He could draw all people to Himself as Savior. Then God exalted Jesus further in the resurrection and ascension.

We also have to leave to God the way and time He will elevate us. Just as God fulfilled His promise to raise His Son (Ps 2), He has given us the promise and has fulfilled that promise through Jesus. God's timing is not up to us.

The Exalted Son, Exalted Name

Not only did God the Father exalt the Son, God gave Him a special name—the Name above every name.

Why did your parents name you as they did?

If you have children, why did you name them as you did?

---

[54] E. W. Bullinger, *Figures of Speech Used in the Bible* (Grand Rapids: Baker Book House, 1968), 429-433.

Possibly you named your child after someone you hoped that child would model. You liked that person, or that personality. In the ancient world, a name related closely to the *nature* or *character* of its bearer. In the case of deity, the name also indicated power.

In the Old Testament, God chose that His name, and therefore His presence and power, would dwell in the tabernacle (Deut 12:11). The Israelites would not pronounce God's name YHWH (יהוה). They would either substitute *Adonai*, or they would refer to *ha-sheem,* the Name, to reverence Him and His power.

Throughout the OT and NT, people pray in the Name. In John 3:17-18, John shows the power of Jesus' name for believers. In His Name they will not be condemned. The Name is not a title but a *synecdoche*, or representation of all God is: His person, presence, character, activity, etc. Through the Name of Jesus, God rescues, saves, and restores. Through that Name and in that Name, we pray. God gives *authority* through the Name of Jesus Christ.[55]

That Name is *beyond* every other name (ὑπέρ again). The Name is perfectly higher than everything in every way. Remember that Christ had that name prior to His incarnation. Equal with God, He shared the rights and traits of YHWH, *the* Name.[56] Believers now can ascribe that name to *Jesus Christ* for the glory of the Father.

When the Lord arose and ascended, He carried the Name *Jesus* Christ into heaven. *Jesus* represents the human side of us. The only way we could get to God was through the incarnational sacrifice which Jesus Christ bought for us. Jesus adds the obedience of His sacrifice to the glory of His God-Man Name. That is why we pray in the name of Jesus.

Hallelujah!! No wonder Paul breaks into song as much as he does!!!

Paul wants his readers to recognize that putting themselves above someone else is the total opposite of Jesus Christ. No matter how high people strive to reach personal exaltation, they will never reach the authority or exaltation of Jesus. We can experience God's glory, authority, and exaltation as He alone chooses to give them to us.

When have you wished you could be better than someone else?

When have you thought you *were* better than someone else?

What does God say about either one of those thoughts?

Philippians 2:10. Paul says when the name Jesus is spoken, everyone will bow.

They will either humble themselves or be humbled. *Every being*[57] will bend the knee before the Lord. Those beings may have already died or may be alive, but wherever they are—in *heaven, on earth*, or *under the earth*—they will bow on their knees.

---

55   See Lenski, *Ephesians and the Philippians*, 157.
56   YHWH is also called the Tetragrammaton.
57   *New Greek-English Interlinear New Testament*, trans. Robert K. Brown and Philip Wesley Comfort, ed. J. D. Douglas (Carol Stream, IL: Tyndale House Publishers, 1990): Philippians 2:10.

Imagine being in a huge stadium full of people and animals in the stands and on the field. Then, imagine all kneeling. How does that make you feel?

Philippians 2:11. Read Isaiah 45:22-24.

Paul echoes Isaiah 45:22-24 in Philippians 2:11.[58] Paul uses the verses in Isaiah to show the parallelism which emphasizes his point. Not only will every knee bow, every tongue will make a confession.

The parallelism, the bowing and the confessing, the use of knee and tongue, fulfills God's plan that every being will honor Jesus totally.[59] Tongue, *glossolalia*, can mean a person's physical tongue or a person's language. Here in whatever language, every person will confess with their tongue instrument.

Read James 3:6-9. How can people use their tongues?

Read James 3:10-11. How should people use their tongues?

No matter how a person's tongue has been used in the past, that instrument will be used to pay tribute to Jesus Christ at the eschaton, the end times. Every tongue will confess, *agree and admit*, that *Jesus Christ* is *Lord*!

Imagine in the stadium with every knee bowed, the chorus of voices saying, "Jesus Christ is Lord!" Does that send chills up and down your spine as it does mine? Spend time exclaiming Jesus as Lord. Maybe you know the song, "He is Lord." This would be a good time to sing it.

No football or soccer team winning a hard-fought tournament will ever experience what Christ will when all acknowledge Him as the Creator in control. Whew!! I'm still tingling!!

Let's look at the meaning of the three terms in this passage—two of these began as titles: Christ and Lord, even though Lord also was the Name in the OT. The two titles originally were considered appositives for Jesus. However, Christ has become a part of His name—no other Name is like His:

Jesus derives from the Hebrew for *Yeshua: the Lord is salvation*.
Christ or *Christos* means *the Anointed One* or *Messiah*.
Lord means *authority* or *master*. In the LXX, this term κύριος, *kurios*, is the name substitution for YHWH and Adoni.

---

[58]   Melick, *Philippians, Colossians, Philemon*, 108.
[59]   Witherington III, *The Paul Quest*, 248.

The church confession in the Greek originally was *The Lord who is Jesus Christ*. Paul uses Lord for Jesus directly applying the *name* from the Septuagint.[60] The future pronouncement will be to the Lord and Master of all, the Anointed One and Salvation for all. For the early church, this expression was a key confession. The terms eventually became the composite name: *the Lord Jesus Christ* and the confession changed to Jesus Christ is Lord.

Read 1 Corinthians 12:3. How could people make such a confession?

Since people can only confess this truth through the power of the Spirit, how can those who do not believe, in the last day profess that the Lord is Jesus Christ?

Even if a person has not believed Jesus is Lord before the end times, that person will *know* the only Lord is Jesus Christ. The Spirit will not be *in them* making that confession *through them*, but will direct their confession through *His power*.

Unfortunately, not all who make that confession will go to heaven on that day. They will realize they denied Him as the ultimate Master, but it will be too late to accept Him as Savior. This eschatological (*end times*) image brings the future into sight: all will acknowledge the Name above all names. At that point, they will recognize Jesus as Judge. Nevertheless, today we can call on that Name above all names as Savior and Lord.

Look at the stadium again. Look at the people in that stadium who did not know Christ as Savior before they knelt on that field or in those stands. How does that make you feel?

Do you have still have joy bumps, or does the reality of their desperate situation change your mind?

What do you need to do to help people change from being in that situation?

Glory to God the Father

The completion of the song in Philippians 2:11 does not end with the honoring of Jesus Christ alone. Whatever is done happens so the Father receives glory. Paul reminds the readers of the equality that began in 2:6. God the Father bestows the Name above all names with the realization the honor points back to Himself.

Read John 17:1, 4, 5, 6, 10, 11, 24. List what these verses say about:

1. The glory of the Father and Son:

---

60   Fee, *Pauline Christology*, 190.

2. The Name:

Notice that in this prayer of John 17, Jesus indicates that whenever He is glorified, the Father receives the same glory. Since Jesus is "the *Father's glory*,"[61] what honor He receives *automatically* belongs to the Father. When the Name of God is mentioned, Jesus is that God. Jesus represents the Tetragrammaton (YHWH) as the Lord, *Kurios*. God chooses to receive His own honor through a full magnification of Christ.[62]

Consider how your life reflects the attitude of Christ and the glory of God. Do you offer humility and praise to God the Father through the Lord Jesus Christ in the power of the Spirit, or do you still grasp onto the glory for yourself?

State here what you would like to do to change in this area.

The term "Jesus is Lord" was a confession which may have been used during the Eucharist as well as at a baptismal service. "Jesus is Lord" still is a confession of the church.

In liturgical churches, the confession may be stated as part of the weekly program. In what are called free churches—churches that may not use the liturgy—the phrase may not be used in the worship services on a weekly basis. Regardless what churches we attend, though, we are to live with Jesus as Lord and confess Him every day.

The term "Jesus is Lord" became a very popular statement in the 1970's when the "Spirit-Filled Life" teaching began to permeate all denominations. Jesus' Lordship became an important topic. Some people in the "Spirit-filled Life" movement taught that we can experience Jesus as Savior, but Lord only later.

However, in reality, He cannot be Savior if He is not Lord. When we surrender to Jesus as Savior, we are saying, "I take you as Lord of my life." We may not understand all that "Lordship" means until later, but He still is Lord. The statement of accepting Christ into our lives as Savior indicates He is saving us from the penalty of sin, the power of sin, and the presence of sin. As Lord, He directs our lives from the initial point of salvation until we get to heaven.

Do we still sin?   Do we still act as if Jesus is not Lord?

Yes, we do. Still sinning does not mean He is not Lord. It means we still need to grow and accept His full rule each day of our lives. New Testament salvation does not mean *we* make Jesus Lord of our lives. We confess He IS Lord, and we live in the light of that truth.

What areas of your life do not reflect Christ in control?

---

[61]   Ibid., 174.
[62]   Schreiner, *Paul, Apostle of God's Glory in Christ*, 182.

Another Look at Philippians 1:27-2:11

Let's return to the issues surrounding 2:6-8 and approach the study in a different comparison. In order to consider what some scholars think is the context of the Hymn, I want to revisit this passage. We will examine 2:6-11 in light of 1:27-2:5. Since Philippians 2:5 is a hinge verse and a key element in the context, let's look at it first.

Reread Philippians 2:5. To what does Paul refer in the first part of verse 5?

Why would Paul command his readers as he does in 2:5? (You might want to return to 1:27-2:4 for help.)

Believers are to:

conduct themselves in a manner worthy of the gospel of Christ, regardless if Paul is
    present or absent (1:27);
stand firm in unity (1:27);
strive together for the faith of the gospel (1:27);
not be alarmed by their opponents (1:28);
remember they have the privilege not only to believe in Christ, but also to suffer for
    His sake (1:29);
experience the same types of conflicts Paul has (1:30);
remember the encouragement they have had from Christ and others (2:1);
make Paul's joy complete (2:2);
consider others better than themselves (2:2-4).

Just like Paul, when believers suffer they testify to the fact that Christ is worthy of such devotion. They willingly give a defense of their faith by offering their lives and possessions. Through this way of life, others may realize the importance of Jesus Christ as Lord.

Paul repeats that the people are suffering in the same way Jesus and he did. Therefore Paul wants them to understand they are not alone in their suffering. Believers need to stand firm individually and collectively. Paul surely implies he has stood firm because Jesus has stood with him. Paul says Christians have the community—if the community will stand firm together. Still, even when an individual has no one else to stand beside him or her, that believer has Christ, Paul, and . . .

Read Hebrews 11:1-12:2. What picture do we have of others standing with us when we go through our trials?

We do not have the witnesses' physical presence. However, the encouragement from their stories, firm stances, and testimonies give us reasons to persevere.

With this in mind, review the command in Philippians 2:5. This verse also implies that a picture of the right attitude is about to come. Paul gives the visual of the attitude in the Christ Hymn. We will look at 2:1-4 alongside 2:6-8.

Believers-Christ Attitude Comparison

2:1-4	2:6-8	Explanations
2:1 If any encouragement in Christ, consolation of love, fellowship of the Spirit, affection and compassion	Existing in the form of God	Remember the Greek word for form indicates *the same as*. Therefore Father, Son, and Spirit fellowship together and fellowship with believers (See John 14:16-31.). The love of God and Christ comes through Christ's emptying Himself for the sake of mankind.
2:2 Being of the same mind, intent on one purpose	2:6-7 Emptying Himself	Jesus and God were intent on the same purpose: the salvation of mankind; believers should have the same humble attitude.
2:3-4 Doing nothing from empty conceit; considering others as more important; not merely looking to one's own interest	2:6-8 Not considering His glory something to grasp; emptying himself; taking the form of a bond-slave	Jesus did nothing from empty conceit—He deserves honor. He emptied Himself of His privileges and took the form of a servant for each of us. He did not look to His own interests of staying in heaven, or dismissing the cross. Remember Him in the Garden of Gethsemane (Lk 22:39-46).
2:4 Looking to the interests of others	2:8 Becoming obedient to death on the cross	Jesus looked to the interests of others by dying on the cross as the perfect sacrifice to redeem mankind. Jesus took this role prior to creation and the incarnation.

Jesus presents the ultimate picture of the right attitude towards others. Because of Jesus' obedience to the plan of salvation, God exalted Him (2:9-11). Jesus Christ presents us with the most vivid picture of what full obedience means.

Possibly after finishing humming the Christ Hymn, Paul considered another song—a song of unity in obedience. Paul would not have considered the commandments of God a burden, but a joy. We can see what Paul thinks about obedience in the next seven verses. We will study the verses in two sections: 2:12-13 and 2:14-18.

A Continued Song of Obedience (2:12-30)

Working with the Lord

We are to obey in the same way Christ did when He went to the cross. We are to obey in the same way Paul did when he served the Lord. Both obeyed in humility, joy, and unity with other believers.

Philippians 2:12-13. The Greek term at the beginning of verse 12 can mean *so then* or *therefore*.

We are familiar with the transition word "therefore." Maybe we have become so used to the word, we do not even stop to see what "therefore" is "there for" anymore. We need to stop, look, and determine the context—where that word points.

In 2:12, the term *therefore* takes us first to 1:27-2:5.[63] In these verses, we are to remember the call to harmony and humility. We are to remember to remain strong and help each other.

Second, the "therefore" reference points forward to the rest of the verses in chapter 2, to the Christ Hymn. Christ's attitude we are to imitate is obedience towards God's will. In that way, we honor God, treat others properly, and witness to the world.[64]

Reread 2:8. What does the verse say about obedience?

Christ's obedience meant He was willing to take *the lowest place*.[65] Remember Christ was already in the highest place. Then God raised Him to that place again with the resurrected body, so we could have a place in heaven. The Lord's humbling of Himself provides us Christians the example and motivation for obedience, and for trusting that God will raise us to a higher place.[66]

Jesus Christ's Spirit would work in the hearts of the Philippians and also will work within us. God's grace may be free, but He expects obedience. Life in community requires each person's obedience for harmony to continue.

Paul calls the believers, "My Beloved." Reread 1:8. Just how much did Paul love the Philippians?

---

[63] Fee, *Paul's Letter to the Philippians*, 230.

[64] Phil. 4:9; A. T. Robertson, *Paul's Joy in Christ; Studies in Philippians* (New York: Fleming H. Revell Company, 1917), 242-243. Paul realized he was the example or "transmitter" of Christ's example to the churches he founded and people he taught; 2 Timothy 1:11-14; Philip H. Towner, *The Letters to Timothy and Titus*, NICNT, eds. Ned NB. Stonehouse, F. F. Bruce, and Gordon D. Fee (Grand Rapids: William B. Eerdmans Publishing, 2006), 456-7.

[65] Karl Barth, *The Epistle to the Philippians* (Richmond: John Knox Press, 1947), 68-69; Moisés Silva, *Philippians* (Grand Rapids: Baker Book House), 134-5.

[66] Fee, *Paul's Letter to the Philippians*, 216.

Paul's love shines through the command he is about to give. Many of us balk at an authority figure giving us instructions. We may even cringe at the Scriptures telling us what to do.

How do you feel when one of the biblical writers uses command language? Check all the answers below that apply to you:

___I immediately stop and ask the Lord to guide me in obeying what the text commands.

___I feel guilty for I know I am not doing what I should in this area.

___I quickly shy away from the command, for I really do not want to do it.

___I think the command applied to the people in the Bible so I do not get too serious about what it says for me.

Paul can command the readers because they would not have a relationship with Christ without the apostle. The Philippians owe Paul a debt. They love him, but they also need to remember what he has done for them in bringing them to Christ.[67] They should take note of *why* he is calling them to obedience as well as *what* he is demanding they should do.

In verse 12, Paul tells *when* the believers should obey. What two times are the followers of Christ to be obedient?

1.
2.

The obedience comes through hearing Paul's instructions, but he no longer is with them. They still are to obey. The attitude of total obedience ("you always obeyed in my presence") is the attitude that must continue in his absence. Just as they shared the gospel from the love of their hearts (1:17), they are to continue to obey in love while he is in prison.[68]

Remember when you were a child and your parents told you to do something. When did you obey better: in their presence or absence?   Why?

Obeying Paul's instructions should not depend on whether Paul was present. Their obedience, and ours, is really for the Lord. Because we are "in Christ," the Holy Spirit lives in us. Therefore, He is always present.

We have all the motivation we need to obey the Lord's commands all the time. We have a promise in verse 2:13 that provides us intrinsic incentive and capability. We will look more deeply at that verse after we consider an excursus on obedience from the OT and NT.

Paul mentions in 1:9, 1:17, 2:2, and 2:4 that the Philippians' love is to become greater and greater. Just as they have shared the gospel in love or experienced the love of God, they are to imitate Christ. Just as Jesus obeyed, they are to obey.

---

[67]   Fee, *Paul's Letter to the Philippians*, 230-231; Fee, *God's Empowering Presence*, 748.

[68]   Barth, *The Epistle to the Philippians*, 68-69; also, see Silva, *Philippians*, 134-35.

Read Paul's commands in Colossians 3:12-14. What does Paul tell us in verse 14?

Again we hear his song about unity. Obedience to love is part of the issue of unity, and therefore joy.

Throughout the NT, the writers underscore their books with the Double Love Command: to love God and neighbors. Paul is no different. He expects the kind of obedience that arises from such love.

Although Paul does not blatantly quote the two greatest commandments in Philippians, we should be able to sum up his understanding of obedience through those commandments. We definitely can when we take into consideration his other letters. As a Jew Paul would have known and expected his readers to understand that they are to love God with all their hearts, souls, minds, and strength, and to love their neighbors as themselves.

An Excursus on Obedience: Loving as God Expects—
The Shema, Decalogue, and Double Love Command

Before we look at the rest of verse 12, let's investigate further the concept of obedience. Often when we think of obedience, we think immediately of the Ten Commandments. Another way of referring to those commands is "The Decalogue." *Decalogue* means *Ten Words* or *Ten Sayings*. Considering obedience to God by observing the Ten Commandments is not entirely wrong, but we should remember two things the Lord taught us about those Commandments.

First, we see how Jesus treated the Commandments in the Gospels and Sermon on the Mount (Mt 5-7). He dealt with the *spirit* of the commands by expanding their meaning to the intents of our hearts.

Second, we find Christ's declaration of the Greatest Commandments or the *Double Love Command* in Matthew, Mark, and Luke. Jesus said all the commands and the whole OT *depend* or *hang* on those two great commandments. In other words, the underlying emphasis of the OT comes in our loving God and neighbors in every way we can. Let's take time to investigate each great command in greater detail.

Love for God

Read Deuteronomy 6:4-6. What is the reason we should love God?

In Hebrew, the word for love is that of pure love. The word aligns with *agape* in the Greek. Our love for God should be the same as God's: self-giving or self-denying. In Deuteronomy, we find the basis for Christ's synopsis of the greatest commandments. When Christ teaches the greatest commandments, He reflects almost entirely on the LXX, but the Septuagint is a translation from the Hebrew. Deuteronomy 6:4-9 is called the *Shema*. The word for *hear* in Hebrew is *shemah* and is the first word in 6:4. The first word in a sentence often is the way a theme is introduced, so Shema describes the liturgy of how the Israelites were to love God in their worship.

The command to hear brought powerful meaning to the Israelite people. When God spoke, they were to listen and obey. From Deuteronomy 6:4, the people should remember that God is the only God so He is the only one who deserves unconditional love from His people. They should remember Him for who He is and for what He has done.

The people usually recited the Shema twice a day in worship.[69] Worship implied love. They were to worship because they loved God, even though He would demand their worship. The requirement to love the Lord echoes in the first three commands of the Decalogue.

Read Exodus 20:2-7. How do these verses compare with the first great commandment?

Do those commands sound negative to you?   Why or why not?

If so, maybe 1 John 4:19 seems more positive. Read that verse. According to John, why do we love God?

Love comes to us from God first. Then we return the love. When we can realize the love of God—as coming from the only all-true, all-wise Creator, the only God who deserves worship, and who CHOSE to design and save us—we cannot view love as just a legalistic emotion, or that the commands are harsh.

Notice the word for love is a verb. God started the action, but expects reciprocity. His laws are for our benefit and the benefit of all mankind. He requires obedience to love because He knows what is best for us.

Reread Exodus 20:2-7. This list is known as the *first table* of the Decalogue. List the ways this passage says we can show our love for God.

Have you ever considered obeying those commands as loving God with your whole person?

Love is vital in our worship. Do you worship the Lord for fear of reprisal or because you love Him?

---

69   Donald A. Hagner, *Matthew 14-28*, WBC 33b, ed. by David A. Hubard, Glenn W. Barker, and Ralph P. Martin (Dallas: Word Books Publisher, 1995), 647.

I used to love the Lord Jesus, but quake before God the Father. Needless to say, my view of God was warped. Then, at a retreat for missionary women in the Philippines, I envisioned God as the Father, *Abba*. He sat on His throne and invited me onto His lap.

Abba wanted to hold me as *His* child. He wanted me to sit on His throne with Him as His little daughter. He wanted me to love Him as a father who is good to me. He wanted me to return His love.

Have you ever seen God as the Father who loves you, or do you think He is the God who makes harsh demands on your life?

We cannot see the love and commandments of God as mutually exclusive. Even though God loves us unconditionally, He has the right to expect our devotion and obedience. Our attitude toward obedience reflects what we think of God and His words.

Read 1 John 5:1. What is necessary in order to love Jesus?

Now, this verse does *not* mean if we do not love the Father appropriately we are not Christians. It *does mean* we certainly have not experienced all God wants us to experience in relationship with Him. It may mean we have not allowed the love of the Father to permeate us with His intimate warmth.

We are about to break down the first great commandment into its four parts and examine each section. The OT mentions three areas of our lives with which we love God. Jesus expands the ways to four (Mk 12:30). However, before we do this, let's look again at how our view of God and His will affects our love.

Read Psalm 119. How does the Psalmist feel about God's commands or law?

List the verses where you get that idea.

Read 1 John 4:9-10, 16-18. Complete the blanks:

Love has _____ _____.

Perfect (mature) love _____ _____ fear.

Fear has _____.

The one who fears is not _____ _____ in love.

Notice the difference between love and fear. Love from God and love for God keep fear from becoming perfect, from maturing or growing. Fear keeps love from maturing us or our confidence. Perfect or mature love drives out fear, expels it. Why would we want to live in fear rather than in love? Obedience to love builds our trust in the One who loves us.

Love with All Our Hearts

We cannot mature in the love of God the Father, Son, and Spirit when we allow fear to rule in our hearts. In that case, fear has become a god. We may often let the god of fear rule our lives and stop us from obeying the only true God. God tells us not to put other gods before Him or make graven images to represent Him. That command includes not making fear our god, even in our worship. We are to respond to His heart with all of our heart.

What other gods do you worship or put before the Father (Maybe it is fear of Him as a terrifying god)?

Write a love letter to God as the Father of love. Confess any inappropriate fear you have of Him or fear of anything else. Ask Him to cradle you and rock you as His child. Ask Him to show you something about Himself and His love which you have not realized before now.

Read Deuteronomy 6:4, Matthew 22:37-38, Mark 12:29-30, and Luke 10:27. Different texts give different lists about love. Some list three items, some four. List the differences in the texts:

Deuteronomy:
Matthew:
Mark:
Luke:

The three or four words actually represent a whole unit. We are not to be divided into parts with one part loving Him more than another. Too often, we may surrender our hearts more to God than our minds or strength, but we are to love Him totally.

With which part(s) do you think you may love the Lord more, or surrender more?

Which part(s) gets less love and attention?
Why?

In the LXX and Greek NT, the word for heart is *kardia*. We recognize the word *cardiac* from this Greek root. In the Hebrew, the word for heart is *lēb* or *lēbbab*.

Say the Hebrew word lebbab several times.

Can't you just hear that word for *heart* as if the heart were pumping? Lebbab, lebbab, lebbab! It sounds as if God has given us an onomatopoeia to remind us that our hearts are to beat for Him. The word for heart here does not mean the physical organ.

Heart stands for the *intelligence, conscience,* or *part that reasons.* Another way of saying this is our *inner life.*[70] The words both in Hebrew and Greek also mean our *mind,* our *will. Lebbab* is a common idiom in Hebrew for the *seat of thought,*[71] or *control center of our human personalities.*[72] We will examine how to love the Lord with our minds later in the study. At this point, we need to examine why we should love the Lord with our *inner life.*

Beside each passage, tell what God's Word says about the heart:

Genesis 6:5:
Matthew 15:18-19:
Psalm 78:8:
Proverbs 12:20:
Jeremiah 16:12:
Jeremiah 17:9:
Jeremiah 23:9:

How in the world, *if our hearts are like that,* can we love God totally with them?

Now beside each passage, write what can happen to our hearts:

Psalm 51:10:
Psalm 69:20:
Proverbs 23:15:
Jeremiah 24:7:

---

[70]   *BDB,* s. v. לֵב.
[71]   R. W. L. Moberly, "Toward an Interpretation of the Shema," in *Theological Exegesis: Essays in Honor of Brevard S. Childs,* ed. Christopher Seitz and Kathryn Greene-McCreight (Grand Rapids: William B. Eerdmans Publishing, 1999), 126.
[72]   Witherington III, *The Paul Quest,* 209.

Read Psalm 66:18. What happens when we do not change our hearts?

Read Psalm 139:23-24. What does the psalmist ask God to do with his heart? List the things he asks the Lord to do:

Notice the synonymous parallelism in these two verses. Synonymous parallelism means the second line says exactly the same thing in another way:

Search me, O God, and know my heart;
Try me and know my anxious mind.

We observe two things here:

First, "O God" is not repeated in the second line. "O God" is not necessary in the second line because the phrase is understood. When something is missing, the term is "ellipsis." We can infer, "Search me, O God, and know my heart; try me . . . and know my anxious mind."

Second, that second line includes an adjective in English which the first does not have in Hebrew.

What is the adjective?

What does that tell us about the psalmist's heart?

For confirmation, see verse 24. What words confirm verse 23?

In the Hebrew, synonymous parallelism is a one-on-one correlation. The Hebrew does not have two words for *anxious mind*, just one. The English must use two. *Heart* and *anxious mind* represent the same thing by using synonyms. Immediately, after declaring his hatred for fickleness, the psalmist then asks the Lord to search his own life for any doubts or double-mindedness.

Reread 139:17-22. How much does the psalmist want to love the Lord?

List the positive words in verses 17-18 that express the psalmist's love.

List the negative words in 19-22 that demonstrate the depth of his love.

Psalm 139:23-24 seem to indicate a contradiction in the psalmist's attitude from 19-22, or that he is repenting of his feelings for the wicked. However, he does not tolerate what the wicked do. The writer knows his thoughts about God must remain proper, so he has to hate what God hates. What the psalmist hates is being "inconsistent, fickle, and double-minded."[73]

So, he asks God to search his mind. The word for *search* (châqar) means *to examine intimately*. One understanding of the word is *probing*, as in a legal investigation—*thoroughly digging into something*. The word for *try* is a mining term. The way metal is *tried* comes through smelting it. Just as we mentioned earlier, when metal is heated, the dross burns off, and the silversmith sees his image.

Therefore, what is the psalmist asking the Lord to do to him?

We do not want to invite trouble, but loving the Lord with all our hearts means a willingness for the Lord to probe deeply. We trust Him to burn off the doubts and dross, and allow His image to shine through us.

Reread Psalm 139:17. What doubts do you have about the Lord's thoughts for you?

What is keeping you from loving the Lord with all your thoughts?

Read 1 Peter 1:3-9. In verses 7-9, list at least three things that *result* from our being tested.

Read 1 Peter 1:22. What does the result of that testing *ultimately* bring?

With *purified souls*, we can love the Lord our God even better. Let us start at the very beginning (literally!), and learn something about the soul.

Love with All Our Souls

---

[73]   *BDB*, שׁנא.

Read Genesis 2:7. What does this passage say man became?

The KJV says God formed man a body, breathed life into him, and man *became* a living soul. The word in the Hebrew here means *soul* or *living being*. We *are* a soul. When we love the Lord our God with all our souls, we love him with our very lives.

Discover some of the characteristics of the soul and what we do with it. Beside each passage, in your own words tell what we can do in our souls:

Job 33:30:
Psalm 24:4:
Psalm 42:1-2; 63:1:
Psalm 62:1:
Ezekiel 18:4:
Matthew 11:28-29:
Matthew 16:26:
Matthew 26:38 (Notice who is saying this.):
Luke 1:46:
John 12:27:
1 Peter 2:11:

Which of these verses troubles you the most and why?

Which of these encourages you the most and why?

How can these characteristics help you love the Lord with all your soul?

In the same way we love the Lord with all our hearts, we love Him with our souls.

Read Jeremiah 29:11-13 and Deuteronomy 4:29. With what are we to seek the Lord?

What happens when we seek Him this way?

Read 1 Peter 2:25. What does this verse say about Christ?

Beside each passage, list what the Shepherd does for us His sheep:

Christ as Shepherd:

Psalm 23:
Psalm 28:9:
Isaiah 40:11:
Isaiah 53:6:
Jeremiah 3:15:
John 10:3:
John 10:7:
John 10:10-11:
Luke 15:6:
Jeremiah 29:13:
> Who really does the seeking?
> What is our part in that?
Revelation 7:17:
Revelation 5:12:
> What did the Lamb do for us?

Christ as Overseer: The term means *guardian*—the one who is to protect and see that things are done correctly.[74] From the context of the biblical text, write what overseers should or should not do:

2 Chronicles 2:18:
1 Peter 5:2-3:

What does Peter say in 5:2 that the overseers of the churches are to be?

The two words shepherd and overseer imply the same thing. A shepherd oversees his sheep. He protects them. He guards their welfare. He makes sure that they go where they should and do not do what they should not.

Read the following passages. How did God guard and guide the people?

Exodus 13:21-22; 14:19-20:
1 Samuel 2:9:
Psalm 25:5:
Psalm 48:14:
Psalm 73:24:
Psalm 141:3:
Isaiah 52:12:
John 16:13:
Philippians 4:7:

---

74   *BDAG*, s. v. ἐπίσκοπος, *episkopos* from which we get the word for *episcopacy* or *elder*.

We love the Lord our God with our whole beings when we trust Him to be our guard and guide. The soul houses the very breath of life. The word for soul involves our personalities, emotions, thoughts, perceptions, appetites or desires, and wills.[75] The soul is the "center" of who we are. When we consider thoughts and perceptions, we usually think of them being from our minds. We will see as we study loving God with our minds just how our minds and souls intertwine.

Read 1 Samuel 18:3. How does Jonathan love David?

The concept here is that soul denotes the personality. Jonathan loved David as if David were the very personality, the very self, of Jonathan.

Read Psalm 42:5-6, 11. What do these verses show about our emotions?

Read James 4:1-10. How does James portray those souls?

Reread 1 John 2:15-17. What does this say about loving the Father?

Read 1 Corinthians 2:14. What is the condition of the person outside of Christ?

Read Ephesians 2:1-3. List the status of our souls these verses describe.

Because of sin, we do not have the capacity to love God with our souls. How we love Him comes from the love of God *in* us. Since Jesus first loved us and put love within us through His Spirit, we can love God in return (Rom 5:5).

Charles Wesley (1707-1788) wrote the hymn, "Jesus, Lover of My Soul," as the Lord was sparing him from an angry mob in Ireland. The people did not appreciate Wesley's teaching on salvation and rushed to kill him. He hid in Jan Lowrie Moore's milk house. As the people got closer, Jan told him to hide in the garden. Near a brook while hiding, Wesley vividly felt the nearness and love of God and composed the hymn. Wesley indicated in the hymn that the Lord hides, supports, comforts, and provides. Jesus is all his soul craves.[76]

Read Psalm 42:1-2. What does the soul seek?

---

[75]   *KBL*, s. v. נֶפֶשׁ. The different connotations are other meanings for *soul*.

[76]   Charles Wesley, "Jesus, Lover of My Soul," [on-line] accessed July 1, 2007, http://www.cyberhymnal. org/htm/j/l/jlmysoul.htm.

How earnestly does the soul want what it seeks?

With the soul as the "center of feelings and perceptions,"[77] i. e. our *emotions*, *longings*, *desires*, or *cravings*, we need to be aware of what we crave. Our desires indicate what we love.

Read the following verses. Beside each one, tell how the soul is involved.

Proverbs 23:1-3:
Ecclesiastes 6:3:
Song of Solomon 3:1-4:

We are to crave or long for the Lord in the center of our lives. We see this in 1 John 2:15-17. John warns us the Lord is to be the one who rules our emotions, cravings, passions, and thoughts.

Love with All Our Minds

When God breathed life into us, His Spirit activated every part of us. We automatically understand that He gave us our minds. However, I wonder how much we dwell on loving God with the intellectual part of our souls, our mental capacities.

Read Job 32:8.[78] What does this verse tell us about the soul?

This is one of the ways we live in the image of God. When God infused us by His Spirit, He also gave the ability and godly wisdom to discern right and wrong. We can distinguish between truth and lies. Our minds have the ability to reason and judge what is right. We can act and interact logically with our ability to reason. We can truly know God and His will.

Read 1 Corinthians 2:9-14. List all the things the Spirit does for us.

Because we have the mind of Christ, we have similar capabilities as He. By no means are we omniscient, but we probably can do a whole lot more than we do now mentally. Someone once said we use the equivalent of the tip of our little finger with our mental abilities, when our whole hand represents the mind God gave us and wants us to use.

What we do with those abilities indicates how well we think and reason as the Lord wants. He desires that we grow in the truth and knowledge He has given us. John Piper indicates that "if we lose the true knowledge of God . . . we lose our ability to reflect his truth and beauty in the world."[79]

---

[77] *KBL*, s. v. נפש.

[78] Davidson, *The Theology of the Old Testament*, 121.

[79] John Piper, "A Mind in Love with God: The Private Life of a Modern Evangelical," an *Outside Events* conference (3 July 1997), under *desiringGod*, http://www.desiringgod.org/ (accessed 13 October 2011). Used by Permission from *desiringGod*.

We need the true knowledge to give us balance in our theology. God calls us to love Him with our minds. We are to involve our emotions *and* our thoughts. Heart without head promotes erroneous emotionalism; head without heart is one-sided dogmatism.

Reread Psalm 139:1-4 and 23-24. What can this tell us about our thoughts?

The psalmist presents an inclusio with those verses. In them, he helps us realize that the Lord can see our thoughts and whether they honor Him. The psalmist wants the Lord to protect his mind from evil thoughts or worrisome thoughts before they become words. At the end of the psalm, just in case he has chosen to have wrong thoughts, the writer wants the Lord to search him and rid him of what thoughts would be wrong. We can ask the Lord to prepare our minds and protect us from wrong thoughts before we think them.

Spend time asking the Lord to prepare your mind for what He wants you to see in this part of the study and to test you for erroneous thoughts. Write what He shows you.

As we have done with our hearts and our souls, let's look at what our minds can do.

Leviticus 24:12:
Numbers 16:28:
Deuteronomy 28:65:
1 Samuel 2:35:
Psalm 31:12:
Proverbs 21:27:
Proverbs 29:11:
Isaiah 26:3:
Lamentations 3:19-24:
Daniel 2:29:
Habakkuk 1:11 (If you have not read this whole book, read it later for the hope in it!!):
Mark 5:15:
Mark 14:72:
Luke 1:8-20, 59-62:
Luke 1:29:
Luke 1:34-35:
Romans 12:16:
1 Corinthians 2:16:
1 Corinthians 3:18-23:
2 Corinthians 8:12:
Philippians 1:27:
Romans 12:1-2:

How does Romans 12:2 fit into the command of 12:1? (When Paul *urges*, he commands.)

What are we to avoid?

Why do our minds need transformation?

How does Paul describe God's will?

As you look at God's will for your life, do you consider it *perfect*? Why or why not?

People often turn to other ways of determining what they are to do. They are willing to buy into other philosophies with astrological signs, Ouija boards, and 8-Balls. Yet they do not allow the Spirit to direct their minds. Even some Christians will turn to those venues for help (Have you read your horoscope in the paper?).

Why do you think people are willing to do that?

Read Leviticus 20:6-8. How does God feel about these things to which people turn?

When Paul says obedience is a reasonable act of service or fits the *regulations for worship*,[80] we have to see obedience as fulfilling God's plans both for worship and for our lives. Fulfilling His perfect will indicates we have a disciplined mind as part of God's perfection for each of us.

God wants us to use the intelligence He created in us. Faith in His will is an informed faith and an intellectual faith. Faith is not a gushy feeling any more than love is. The feelings may be there, but we are to love and believe rationally.

I am about to be blunt. While I really don't want to be arrogant or judgmental, I may sound that way when I say many Christians today are anemic in their study of God's Word and in their study about God. I can sound militant when I wish more Christians had a personal Bible study time *every day*.

Some people do not think it is necessary to dive more deeply into Bible studies since they think they are just fine spiritually. Some people may take their pastor's or teachers' word and not study for themselves. Some people are afraid to study "theology." Let's see what Paul says about that idea.

---

80   *BDAG*, s. v. λατπεία.

Read Acts 17:1-15. Notice the difference in 17:4-5 and 11-12. How did the Bereans handle Paul's and Silas' preaching?

Do you follow the Bereans' way of dealing with what they heard? Why or why not?

Read Proverbs 1:7. What does this say about knowledge and instruction?

What does Solomon call the person who does not take learning about God seriously?

Read 2 Corinthians 10:3-6. How do we defeat those teachings which go against the Lord?

Both OT and NT Scriptures teach that we are responsible to use our minds wisely. We are to take every thought captive to Christ. We are to develop our minds so we live wisely in today's world.

Have you ever been told that people do not like a person who is smart?

What reasons were you given for that statement?

In today's culture, we sometimes hear if we appear too smart, we make other people think they are dumb. We hear that "truth is relative," so we can be satisfied with anybody's idea of truth. We hear we do not have to search too deeply for accuracy.

Surely we should be kind and not hurt peoples' feelings, or display arrogance. Those attitudes violate the very teaching about humility we already have discussed. However, the Lord does hold us accountable for what He has given us—our talents, gifts, abilities, and intelligence.

Why do you think we are we willing to accept the ideas that we should not look too intelligent and we cannot really know truth anyway?

One philosophy indicates no one can really know anything well and that truth is defined by society.[81] Such a mindset brings us the idea that all roads lead to God and anybody's idea of religion is fine. D. A. Carson, a well-known philosopher, says people today are willing to believe:

---

[81]   Larry S. McDonald, *The Merging of Theology and Spirituality: An Examination of the Life and Work of Alister E. McGrath* (Lanham, MD: University Press of America, Inc., 2006), 85. McDonald is using material from one of Millard Erickson's books.

that any notion that a particular ideological or religious claim is intrinsically superior to another is *necessarily* wrong. The only absolute creed is the creed of pluralism. No religion has the right to pronounce itself right or true, and the others false, or even . . . relatively inferior.'" Societal trends include ideas such as "secularization;" "self-awareness, self-fulfillment, and self-actualization;" "Biblical illiteracy;" a cosmic Christ;" "individualism;" and "Freudian ideals."[82]

These pluralistic thoughts can result in a lack of truth—a lack of true knowledge—in our lives. Remember that Paul says in Philippians 1:9 that our love is to grow in *real* knowledge more and more. We only can know real knowledge about God by studying the Bible with more than a surface interest.

How does surface thinking and studying affect our homes, churches, and world?

In order to be all Christ wants us to be and to follow His pattern, we must be aware whether we have accepted the world's pattern of shallow thinking about God.

Reread Galatians 4:19. What is our form?

Read Colossians 1:27-28. What is our hope?

What are we to do according to Colossians 1:28?

Read 2 Timothy 2:14-18. How can we do what Colossians and 2 Timothy tell us, if we do not develop our minds?

If we are not willing to study deeper to be approved, what does that tell God about our love for Him?

God designed us with an intellect so we could love Him in the very best way possible. What we choose to do with our minds affects who we are and how we act. Loving God with our minds and studying His word influences what concepts we accept. Alexander Hamilton once said, "Those who stand for nothing fall for anything." We may think our walk with God is strong enough that we would not fall for other philosophies, but how many of us actually have, because we have not studied the Bible for ourselves?

For example, I have heard many people say, "God helps those who help themselves." They think that is a verse from Scripture. That statement is not Scripture. That statement comes from Benjamin Franklin and it does not agree with what God teaches. We are to depend on the

---

[82]   Ibid., 86.

Lord. Therefore, knowing God's Word is important to keep from accepting wrong philosophies, theologies, actions—and even wrong "quotes."

We can be like the Bereans, like the pattern Paul develops in Romans 12:1-2. We can accept the pattern Paul exemplifies. On the other hand, we can be like people in Thessalonica who did not want their beliefs changed.

Read 1 Corinthians 2:6-16. What does this say about our minds?

Does this affect what you believe about studying the Bible in more depth?

What beliefs, attitudes, and actions have you had to change in your life already?

Have you considered that when God transforms your mind, the change would permeate other areas of your life?

What are you struggling to change right now?

In Romans 12:1-2 Paul sets up the rationale that we allow the Lord to transform our minds so He can change our lives. If our beliefs touch every part of us, then we must develop our intellect—the mind of Christ in us (1 Cor 2:16)—so each area of our lives reflects the image of Christ.

What happens when we do not develop our minds, or feed them intellectually?

Emily Barnes of *More Hours in My Day* has said that if we feed ourselves physically the way we feed ourselves spiritually, we will starve to death.[83] Feeding ourselves spiritually involves feeding our minds. If we do not nourish our intellect, we do not sustain our souls. We can become spiritually and mentally malnourished—or anemic as we said earlier.

What else would this deficiency affect?

If we neglect our souls, our intellectual well-being, we affect ourselves spiritually, emotionally, and physically. We have to make our minds become all they can so we grow in a healthy manner.

Some intellectuals do not believe Christians can think. I have had several people over the years find it astonishing that I was a mathematician *and* a devout Christian. The mind God gives us lets us perform well in all walks of life. We need to know why we believe what we believe intelligently about Jesus.

---

[83] Emilie Barnes, *More Hours in My Day* conference (Riverside, CA, 1980). Used by permission from Emilie Barnes.

We should be able to say why we believe so others accept that God is the all-knowing God. Our minds need continual development, no matter how old we are or how long we have been believers. We continually nurture our minds.

My mother had Alzheimer's Disease for nineteen years. Watching her mind waste away made me realize I need to do whatever I can to prevent that disease from leaving me an empty shell. I may not be able to use the PhD degree I am pursing as long as I would like since I am an older Christian. For as long as possible, though, I can further my mind and worship the Lord intellectually *and* emotionally. *Remember the two do go together*. We all may have many different reasons for improving our minds, but the greatest should be our love for God.

When we are more involved with the world's view of things, we may be satisfied filling our minds with stuff other than what God wants for us. We may satisfy our cravings for food, things, entertainment, and people of this world, rather than God's best. Those other things do not satisfy like God does. God intellectually stimulates us when we study His word. The Lord does not say we cannot have fun and enjoy life, but what we do and why we do those things reflect our priorities.

How do our priorities influence other people?

If changes in our minds can affect other parts of us, how do you think what we believe can affect other peoples' lives?

The changes God makes in us can help alter the lives of people around us. We should care about improving our minds for the good of others, because we have a responsibility to teach others about Christ. Our mission to share the gospel is influenced and affected by our minds. When we study God's word, people can recognize the value of studying.

However, if people see us being satiated with less than God's best, we are not good witnesses in developing our hearts, souls, or minds. Even in Christian material, self-help books should not be our only feeding trough. We need to seek the Lord's guidance to change what we study. The change includes working hard at being better students, intellectuals, writers, and even speakers. We need to develop speaking skills so we articulate the truth of God well.

Name intellectual goals you are willing to set and why you would choose them.

Have things gotten in your way and prevented you from fulfilling your goals or dreams (I have wanted to pursue a PhD most of my life, but I let other peoples' opinions get in my way.)?

Have you let things or people keep you from improving?

Read the following passages. What do they say about some of these issues?

1 Corinthians 2:9-16:

John 14:26:

Philippians 4:8-13:

2 Timothy 1:5-7:

When I tell people I am studying theology, I get mixed reactions. Some say, "That's wonderful!" Others tell me, "Oh that is a deep subject."

To study theology means we are studying about God. Theo-ology is the study of God. Remember –ology = *the study of*. Theos = *God*. If we want to interpret God's Word and know God correctly, we should cultivate our minds in studying about God as much as possible.

Do you believe as a church we truly accept the deep things of God's Word? Why or why not?

How can you help others want to study God's Word more seriously?

How do you see this Bible study helping you in preparation for any other Bible lesson or sermon?

How has this study helped you in your personal quiet time each day?

How has this study changed areas in your daily life?

What new habits do you need to form to study better?

As we have seen, all of us need to grow in our relationship with the Lord. Not everybody needs to pursue a PhD in theology, but we all have things we can do to improve our minds. Just as we increase our mental capacities by reading more difficult books, taking courses in new subjects, or learning more about our favorite interests, we can enhance our aptitude of the Bible. Studying the Scriptures along with commentaries, biblical dictionaries, and Bible atlases can give us greater insight. We also can take courses on the Bible through Christian colleges near us or online.

Loving the Lord through Reason

Read Job 13:3, 15, and 15:3. What word do the verses have in common?

How is the word used in each verse?

Now read Job 23:7, Isaiah 1:18, and Genesis 20:16. List how the word is used in these verses?

The word, in both Hebrew and in Greek,[84] means *to reason, engage in debate,* or *bring proof.* In Job 13:3, the verb is a form which gives the meaning *to argue with, to prove.* The Greek word also can mean *to bring to light, reprove,* or *correct.* In the Isaiah and Genesis passages above, a different verb form indicates that the person *reasons* to *set something right.*

Read 2 Timothy 4:2. What word do you see in that verse?

Reread 1 Peter 3:15-16. List the commands.

Read Matthew 5:13. How does saltiness fit into our line of thinking here?

Read Matthew 10:16-20. What does this passage say about being ready to give an answer?

What do all these verses say concerning what the Lord thinks of logic?

Read Matthew 22:15-22. What did Jesus use to answer the question?

We have read passages that say we can have Jesus' kind of discernment. Jesus used logic to discern, answer, or *argue* with His opponents on several occasions. These opponents were the religious intellectuals who studied a lot. The passages above should encourage us to study and learn to model three things:

    a.   Jesus listened through the Spirit for discernment;

    b.   He applied intelligence appropriately;

---

[84]   The word is יכח in Hebrew and ἐλέγχω in Greek.

    c.   He loved the people with whom He reasoned.

Read Acts 17:1-3, 16-17. What did Paul do in Thessalonica, Athens, and other places?

Where and how often did he do this?

Why did Paul express things the way he did in verse 3?

Why did Paul express things the way he did in verse 16?

Read Acts 17:4, 18-34. Did Paul accomplish his purpose?   Why or why not?

Read 2 Timothy 2:23-25. What can we see about the type of arguments we are to develop?

You have already read several verses that, along with 2 Timothy 2:23-24, indicate what kinds of arguments to *avoid*. In what kind of debate are we *not* to engage?

What is the difference?

Reread 1 Peter 3:1-16. What is our purpose for logic?

What we see in all these verses is that God calls people to engage in reasoning, in higher-order thinking skills.

If you have a computer, search for "Bloom's Taxonomy." You may find two versions. What are the top three levels of both versions?

Generally the webpages give definitions for the terms. What is the meaning of the term "evaluate"?

What other descriptions do you see at that level?

How do the meanings and words fit with our study on reasoning?

Teachers have used Bloom's guide for years to make sure students perform at the top of the chart rather than always staying towards the bottom. Professors know how important it is to help students rise to higher expectations—to meet the top three levels of thinking. For teachers to do otherwise is a disservice. Those scholars realize the importance of developing intellect and reason. How much more would the God who created our minds want us to use them to their highest potentials!

I realized early in my secondary teaching career that when I raised my expectations for my students, they rose to those expectations. All good teachers try to get students to interact through higher thinking, argumentation, and discussion. Interrelating with others' views and helping others grow in reasoning skills is a way to help them develop their minds. We expect that of teachers. We should expect that of ourselves.

Reread 1 Peter 3:15. What are we to do when someone asks why we believe as we do?

The English word for *answer* in the Greek is *apologia*. We get the word *apologize* or *apologetic* from that Greek word. The term does not mean we have to apologize for being a Christian, but we can *give a justification* of our faith.

The word means *to give a defense* or *reason* for *why* we believe *what* we believe. As a woman, I heard for years that men want a woman who is not too intelligent but who is willing to use her body more than her mind. As we mentioned earlier, some people buy into the idea they should not be too smart because it is not popular. *Those ideas are not what God wants for us.* They do not help us know how to share our faith adequately.

Who used logic to help you come to Christ or grow in Him?

Did you realize the person was employing logic to help you understand?

How do you feel about improving your logic and reasoning skills?

We should not be afraid to use reasoning with our faith because we use those skills every day. When I taught mathematics, I constantly got the question, "When are we ever going to use this stuff?" I would tell my students that even if they did not measure angles or work with algebra, geometry, or calculus every day, they used the skill of problem solving all the time. Problem solving involves logic.

Think of times you use logic. How can you improve those skills to help others grow in love for God?

Loving God in Families

Compare 1 Peter 3:2 and 3:15. What word do those verses have in common?

How should the quiet spirit and the solid apologetic work together?

Had you ever considered 1 Peter 3:1-2 and 3:15-16 as part of the same chapter, and therefore, the same intent of the author?   What do you think now?

The word for *respect* in both verses is φόβος, *phobos*, the word from which we get the English word *phobia* for *fear*. The concept in both verses is that men *and* women demonstrate respect for other people when they discuss why they believe in Jesus Christ. That kind of respect applies in the home, church, and world and not just when we are witnessing to someone about Jesus. Our lives should reflect respect.

The issue is not that only men should use logic and women shouldn't. The issue is the best logic to use at the time. Both men and women have God's encouragement to think and discuss well.

Argument does not mean being *argumentative* or *hostile*. An argumentative behavior will never reach another person's mind and heart in the same way that gentleness and respect will. Gentleness does not mean weakness of heart or mind. Gentleness involves humility.

Read James 1:21 and 3:13. What do these verses add to our logic?

Read Ephesians 4:2, Galatians 5:23, Colossians 3:12, Titus 3:2, and 1 Peter 3:16. What do these Scriptures say about *all* believers?

The Greek word in James 1:21 and 3:13 is the same as in Ephesians 4:2, Galatians 5:23, Colossians 3:12, Titus 3:2, and 1 Peter 3:16. We do not lose gentleness when we use logic. Argument means engaging our minds in analysis and discovery of truth for ourselves. Jesus and Paul used the method of argument, of reasoning, to help people see the truth. They engaged other peoples' minds.

How does that apply to men and women using logic?

Does this change how you have interpreted 1 Peter 3:1-4?

What do you think would happen if both women and men used logic in discussions with each other, especially with their spouses?

Does that seem to disagree with the "quiet and gentle spirit" of 1 Peter 3:1-6?

What positive outcome could happen if godly women today studied and loved the Lord more with their minds and developed their inner adornment in the center of their lives?

How do you think that might affect their husbands?

What would happen if men encouraged their wives to study more?

Read Ephesians 5:21, 25-27. How would reassuring wives to study more deeply fit into this picture of Christ loving the church?

How do you think motivating wives to study and reason would affect the women themselves?

How would wives' studying and reasoning affect the children?

Read Proverbs 31:10-31. What does this passage say about a woman who has developed her mind?

List the verse numbers. Beside each verse, give your reason that proves she did develop her mind.

What did her husband and children think of her mindset?

Read Ephesians 6:4. How do you think using logic would help avoid anger in the children?

How do all the verses above apply to self-worth: of men, women, and children?

How can engaging in reason and logic affect our personalities in a positive way?

We believers today need to develop our minds so we can help others see the truth: in God's Word, about who Jesus is, and of Christianity's truth claims as the best way to believe. We simply put logic and argument into proper perspective of respect.

Loving God Mentally All the Time Everywhere

Since logic affects every part of our lives and we use it to help others, we need to realize how to use it in the church. Loving God mentally includes how we act in worship. Remember we should not take what we read and hear corporately without checking for ourselves. We have the responsibility to check for truth, just as the Bereans did. We need to study so we not only grow individually, but so we add to the study and worship of others.

Have you ever considered that by not growing intellectually you affect personal and corporate worship?

How do you feel about that last question?

We already have seen how not developing our minds can affect our quiet time with the Lord and affect the beliefs of others. What we know and accept shows how we handle ourselves in corporate study and worship.

People observe our worship. We are not to worship so they see and praise *us*. We are to consider whether they see us as people who develop our minds even for worship.

How do you think the mind affects *koinonia* or godly fellowship?

What is the strength of your fellowship mentally?

When we develop our love for the Lord, we develop the strength of our fellowship. We also develop strength throughout our whole lives.

Love with All Your Strength

Let's look at two concepts of loving God with our strength: our physical bodies and our determination. We need strength of body as well as strength of character, heart, and soul.

Loving the Lord with the Strength of Our Bodies

The two greatest commandments do not explicitly mention the body with which we are to love God. We have heard we are to love with our *might*, or *strength*. The Hebrew word for *might* does indicate we are to love God with our bodies, *and* all the power within us. We are to love through "the physical side with all its functions and capabilities,"[85] and we are to love like that abundantly.

In Deuteronomy 6:5 we see that what we do with our bodies affects our attitudes about God. We are to love with the "'dynamic of our actions"[86] or the "sum of the energies, bodily and mental."[87] Whatever we do with our bodies, we are to be holy. We cannot live in any way that dishonors God.

Both the OT and NT teach that we should honor God in every way possible. We demonstrate love for Him and others by what we do with our bodies. Romans 12:1-2 teach that our bodies are part of our service and worship to the Lord. We studied the Romans passage for our minds; now, we will use those verses for our bodies. Areas in which we are to be holy include how we express that holiness with our bodies, how we act with our bodies, and how we take care of our bodies.

How We Express Holiness with Our Bodies

Reread Romans 12:1-2. What are we to do with our bodies?

---

[85] Eugene H. Merrill, *Deuteronomy*, NAC 4, ed. E. Ray Clendenen and Kenneth A. Matthews (Nashville: Broadman & Holman, 1994), 164.

[86] John C. Maxwell, *Deuteronomy*, The Preacher's Commentary Series 5, ed. Lloyd J. Ogilvie (Nashville: Thomas Nelson Publishers, 1987), 117.

[87] W. L. Alexander, *Deuteronomy*, The Pulpit Commentary, eds. H. D. M. Spence and Joseph S. Excell (New York: Funk and Wagnalls, 1950), 119.

Read Romans 12:1 and Genesis 4:3-8. How do sacrifices reflect love?

Read Exodus 12:5. What does this tell us about the condition of any sacrifice?

How do Romans 12:1 and Exodus 12:5 concern *us*?

Read 1 Corinthians 3:1-17 and 6:12-20. What are we called?

In 1 Corinthians 6:13-15, Paul mentions why we are to guard what we do with our bodies. What three reasons does he give?

1.
2.
3.

Read 2 Samuel 7:13. What else is in the temple?

Read Genesis 2:7. With this Genesis passage and the other verses above, think about the temple in this way:

a. We are the temple which God formed with His hands;
b. We are the temple of the Son in whose image we are made;
c. We are the temple in whom the Holy Spirit dwells.

What does that do for you intellectually?

How does all this apply to loving God with our bodies?

Let's look at the temple from a different perspective, but one that still involves our bodies:

Read Exodus 28:1-14, 40-43. Why were the garments made?

What did these garments look like?

What happened if the priests went into the tabernacle without appropriate clothing?

Read 1 Peter 2:9-12 in light of Exodus 28. With whom does Peter compare us?

Gentlemen and Ladies, how does your clothing reflect your priesthood and holiness to others—inside and outside the church?

Read 1 Peter 3:3-4. How does what we wear affect the people around us (Guys, consider this too!)?

We have seen in Philippians 1 and 2 that we are to love God and not reflect the world's values. We are to look out for the welfare of others. What we wear can honor God or resemble the world's idea of fashion.

Do you wear clothing that could be a stumbling block to another person?

If you are not sure, think about what clothing causes you impure thoughts and see if you have any clothes that might trigger that problem in someone else. Ask yourself if what you wear is too revealing of some body parts. I am not suggesting that we police what others wear to church. A judgmental attitude could keep them from returning to our churches.

What we need to consider is whether anything *we* do is a stumbling block to someone else's worship or lifestyle. I realize that almost anything we wear might be someone's excuse to stumble or have wrong thoughts. That is not what I mean here. Sometimes we are not aware that we help other people dishonor God with their bodies—we wear things that cause them to struggle sexually, or we imply such clothing is okay.

After reading the section above, some of you may want to say, "Judge not, lest you be judged," or "People look at the outside, but God looks at the heart." Consider the following verses:

James 2:1-7. What do these verses say about clothes?

1 Samuel 16:6-14. What is the issue here?

Galatians 5:1. How does this passage describe us?

We are not to show favoritism toward people because of their dress. We are to treat all people equally with respect. Both the James and 1 Samuel passages speak against placing more value on people who are rich or handsome. We are not to judge people in how they look.

We are free to choose how we look. Freedom, though, brings responsibility and accountability to be holy always. Holiness includes our choice of clothing. Modesty is a virtue we are to pursue. We should not take our cues from the secular society. We can ask the Lord for guidance in how to honor Him with our clothing choices.

Although this discussion about clothing may seem a stretch on the issues of obedience and love, I believe we have an opportunity to love the Lord by living distinctly from the world. If unbelievers cannot recognize a different lifestyle, they may not see how Jesus can affect their lives. We are *free* in Christ, but we also are *set apart* by Christ. I am not suggesting we should be legalistic, but we can appear more modest than what the world says is fashionable. Because we in the church have tried to be less legalistic and more open to peoples' needs, some of us have stopped teaching about lifestyle choices which imitate a society where "anything goes."

As a former teacher, I had the job of enforcing the dress codes of the schools. Several students came dressed inappropriately. They wanted to appear like people in magazines and movies and got upset at the schools' insistence on modesty. When talking with the parents, I noticed occasionally there was little difference in the adults' choices of clothing from what their kids were wearing. The adults needed to realize their kids' vulnerability to succumb to pressure about clothing selections. I heard parents say they did not want to fight their kids in the stores, so they just bought what the kids demanded.

The worldly mindset has moved into the church. The question we need to ask is whether we want to model *anything* that does not reflect a holy picture of Christ in our lives. We may have difficulty buying modest clothing, but we need to search for good styles. Our choices may reveal something we do not intend.

How We Act with Our Bodies

Some of our clothing may offer a view of a lifestyle we would not want people to think we live. Some clothing points to loose idea of sexuality. We are to be pure in our minds and actions toward people of both genders.

Read 1 Corinthians 6:12-20. What do these verses say about our bodies as the temple of the Spirit?

Many Christians today do not think living together outside of marriage is a problem with God. What do verses 16 and 20 say?

We looked earlier at Galatians 5:19-21. What do those verses saying about sexuality? List all words that apply.

Read Psalm 19:8, 25:15, 101:2-4; Proverbs 6:25; Matthew 5:28; Romans 1:24-27; Galatians 5:16; Philippians 3:18; 1 Peter 1:13-16; and, 1 Peter 4:3-4. What is the major thought of these verses?

With 70% of men in general—65% of men in the church—and with 30% of women viewing pornography, we need to change what we set before our eyes. We are to *set* our minds on things above. What we watch affects our feelings about sexuality. In the Sermon on the Mount, the Lord told everyone—not just men—that to lust for someone is the same as committing adultery. Our bodies, as temples of the *Holy* Spirit, must not include anything that will cause us to lust sexually for someone else.

Reread the last word in the fruit list of Galatians 5:23. How would that word apply to holiness before God and others?

How willing are you to love the Lord with your body and be distinctive by changing what you wear, what you see, and how you act (or as 1 Peter 2:11 says, abstain from fleshly lusts which wage war against our souls)?

How We Take Care of Our Bodies

Of particular interest to me is the issue of *rest*. Most of us live in a rapidly-paced society. Too often, we accept the mindset that we must be involved in everything around us. I have had to make a serious evaluation about this in my own life, because I easily can put too much on my schedule.

Read Matthew 11:28-29. Why is it important to love God through rest?

Take time and do a concordance search on the word *rest*. List several Scripture passages here:

You may have found many places where the biblical writers have commanded us to rest. God knows what happens when we do not take periodic breaks. We need to incorporate a time-out periodically, so we can better love the Lord with our strength. Too often we fill our lives with busy-ness and think we honor God with all we do. We pass that attitude to our children. We expect that of other people, especially in the church. Doing too much not only diminishes our strength, the activity also takes our focus away from what God really wants for us. As my missionary prayer partner once told me, "Sometimes rest is the most spiritual thing we can do." Loving the Lord includes giving ourselves time to rest, so we revive our strength and renew fellowship with Him.

Christ formed us for Himself and our might derives from that knowledge. Our strength also becomes better from resting. We need to ask the Lord what we should remove from our schedules so we can rest more.

Other areas of concern for our bodies include eating correctly and exercising properly. These subjects are touchy because we may not want to be convicted about them. Still, we have to reflect the control of Christ on our lives in these issues.

Read Deuteronomy 21:20, Proverbs 23:21, Proverbs 20:1, Matthew 11:19, Luke 7:34, and Titus 1:10-2:15. What do all of these verses tell us about taking care of our bodies?

What verses affect you the most about taking care of yourself and why?

When we do not care for our bodies, we may not realize how we possibly demonstrate a lack of love for our Creator (Tit 1:16; 2:6). We should have the mindset that loving God with our bodies is important. Therefore we may need the strength of determination to help us live distinctively in all parts of our lives.

Loving the Lord with Determination

Loving the Lord with our strength includes loving the Lord with determination to stand firm in doing His will. This concept appears in Paul's appeal of Philippians 1:27-2:11. His thoughts about standing firm resonate throughout the letter. Each of the following passages teaches how determination honors the Lord.

Read Joshua 4:3, Judges 7:2, 4-8, and Nehemiah 2:11-17. What does the Lord tell these men?

How did they honor the Lord through determination?

Read Psalm 18:29. How can this verse help you in the area of strength?

Now read Psalm 18:25-29. Does the context of this passage make a difference?

If we are to love God with all our strength, what else is necessary for loving Him?

Does verse 27 remind you of another one we already studied?   Which one?

Now read Psalm 18:30-36. What does this tell us about our strength?

When the Lord gives the strength, what can we do?

Read 1 Peter 5:5-9. What correlations do you see between these verses and Psalm 18:30-36?

Read 2 Kings 23:24-25. How did King Josiah turn to the Lord?

What do these two verses in Kings tell you of God's thoughts about Josiah?

We see a wonderful model of loving the Lord. Josiah loved Him—with all his heart, soul, and might. Josiah loved the Lord with the *strength of resolve*. He determined to return the people to a right relationship with God. We are to love the Lord with that kind of fortitude so our lives reflect the strength God gives us.

Now read 2 Kings 23:1-23. What do these verses that tell us about loving the Lord with our might?

Read John 16:12-15. What does verse 13 say the Spirit will do in us?

Verse 14 says it is important that we do not study or hear the Word in our own power. Why?

Who is involved when the Spirit is instructing us?

If we do not love the Lord with all our might, with all our forcefulness, we may not *hear* His Word correctly. We cannot *accept* the Word properly in our own strength. We cannot *understand* the Word in our own strength (Remember Deut 6:4 and 1 Cor 2:14-15.). Our lives, hearing, preaching, and teaching are affected when we do not love with all our strength. Our witness can fail—just as it did for the Israelite army against the Philistines.

When we work in our own strength, we work in the flesh. The Bible says a lot about living or working in the flesh versus in the Spirit. At this point, the flesh does not mean our bodies. It means working without the strength and power of the Spirit.

Read Galatians 6:8-9. In the table below, list the differences between working in the flesh and in the Spirit.

Flesh	Spirit

Read Romans 8:5-13. When we live according to the flesh, what happens to our loving God (v. 5)?

List four things mentioned in verses 8:6, 7, and 8 about dwelling on the flesh:

8:6:
8:7a:
8:7b:
8:8:

Reread Romans 8:5. If we love the Lord with our entire being, where do we have to set our minds?

Read Romans 8:11, Colossians 3:1-3, and Ephesians 2:6. What is the common theme in these verses?

Let's do a play on a word here: what we can learn about *set*.

We can see that we are to set the focus of our minds in the heavenlies;
We are to let them stay there, as if set in stone;
We should have the mind-set about God's will that happens in heaven.

What set means is we realize our minds already exist with Jesus in heaven. His death, resurrection, and ascension bought us that privilege. We purposely focus on what is above rather than our current situation. We adopt the mindset that God wants—what people in heaven would understand about God's plan, His love, and our circumstances. Setting our minds in the heavenlies means we recognize God's strength in our lives.

What happens to our strength when we believe differently than this about God?

We have the resurrection life. We have the mind of Christ. We serve Christ in the Spirit. We cannot begin to love the Lord our God with all our minds, our hearts, our souls, *and our strength* if we do not set our minds on things above. *Setting our minds above* means we get rid of what keeps us from living in agreement with God and from living in a weakened condition.

Reread Romans 8:11-13. Go back to what things you might be doing that could be a stumbling block. Now read 8:15. What makes you think you might be living with the world's view instead of a heavenly one?

Do you think being freed from slavery to sin (8:15) gives you permission to do anything you want?

Read Romans 6:1-9, 12-13, 17-22. Whose slave do you want to be?

Every day we must solve this slave issue in our lives. Read Romans 5:1 and 6:3. What do the verses say about our sin?

Ask the Lord to show you how you still act as a slave to sin. Ask him to guide you in loving Him and others. This is *not* to beat yourself up, but to encourage a greater love life with the Lord. Jot notes so you remember in the future what the Lord has told you.

Minds together with Bodies

Let's return to loving God with our bodies. Let's check Romans 12:1-2 again. By now you may be able to recite those verses, even if you had not memorized them earlier! Some might wonder if we are studying Romans instead of Philippians. These two verses in Romans can really give us insight about love in obedience.

Return to Romans 12:1-2. What do they say about the whole issue of loving God?

Ben Witherington III writes about the social life represented in the biblical books. In his study on Romans, Witherington implies from Romans 12:1-2 that "the audience must offer themselves up to God. In fact, Paul will say that they must offer their very bodies up to God, for their bodies are the vehicles through which they act and behave in various ways."[88] In the old covenant of sacrifice, the animal replaced the person. Christ then substituted Himself for each sacrifice. God does not accept any substitutes we humans might try to make, unless He has ordered us to give Him something different. He told us to give our whole selves to Him.[89]

---

[88]   Witherington, *Paul's Letter to the Romans*, 284.
[89]   Ibid., 282.

Such a gift is our spiritual and "reason-able" act of worship. The Jerusalem Bible states the gift as "worship worthy of thinking beings."[90] Here we see our minds and bodies in concert for loving God.

Read 1 Thessalonians 3:2, 12-13; 2 Thessalonians 2:16-17; 3:3, 5; and, Ephesians 3:14-19. What does strength have to do with love in these verses?

Give at least seven reasons strength should increase:
1.
2.
3.
4.
5.
6
7.

What is the ultimate goal of *our hearts* being strengthened?

Read 2 Thessalonians 3:3-5 together with Romans 5:3 and James 1:3. What word does each of these passages have?

The Greek word in all three passages for patience, endurance, or perseverance is ὑπομονή: *hypo + mone, to remain under.* We remain under the trials in order to persevere, because we have the Lord strengthening our hearts. When our hearts are strong, we can be more obedient to honor Him by our actions.

Love for People

The proper view of God means our minds and actions should adjust in attitude towards other people. As we saw in 1 Thessalonians 3:12-13, we are to increase and abound in love for everyone, so that our hearts are holy and blameless when Jesus returns. In Romans 12:1-15:13, Paul dictates how believers should act towards each other *and* non-believers. Our mindset towards God *sets* our minds toward people: as God would think of them.

Reread Philippians 2:6-8. How did Jesus love others as Himself?

Reread Matthew 22:34-40, Mark 12:28-31, and Luke 10:25-37. We are to love first God, then others, but what happens when we reverse the two?

---

[90]   Ibid., 285.

Read Romans 13:9. In light of Philippians 2:6-8, what does the Romans verse say about loving others?

Does this sound like a contradiction?   Why or why not?

Read Romans 12:3. What does Paul expect us to think about ourselves?

Our view of ourselves should not be too high or too low. How we feel about ourselves—our self-worth—determines how well we relate to people. In today's culture, many Christians prefer the word *self-worth* rather than *self-esteem*. The former involves seeing ourselves as the Lord sees us, rather than "esteeming" ourselves too highly. We realize our value through Christ. (Remember Philippians 2:3-4.)

Romans 12:1-3 represents a mini-Double Love exposé. We know we are to offer ourselves first to God (12:1-2). Then in 12:3 we see how we are to think of others.

From Romans 12:3, list the four ways Paul talks about thinking.
a.
b.
c.
d.

The root word is the same for all four words for think in Greek. Paul uses a play on words to tell his readers that people should *not to think too highly* of themselves.

Even though the Greek may be "Greek to you," let's look together at the symbols below to recognize how Paul uses the root word *phroneo*, *to think*.

Look at the way the words line up in the *middle of the verse* and notice the root:

μὴ ὑπερ**φρονεῖν**	he should not *think* of himself more highly
παρ' ὅ δεῖ **φρονεῖν**	than he ought to *think*
ἀλλὰ **φρονεῖν**	but he should *think*
εἰς τὸ σω**φρονεῖν**,	to have sound *thinking* (a sound mind).

Paul begins and ends Romans 12:3 with the only way a person can think properly about other people. The verse literally means:

"Through the grace given to me, I say to every one of you that he should not think of himself more highly than he ought to think, but he should think to have sound thinking as God has allotted to everyone the measure of faith."

The bookends show that God gives us both the grace and the faith to think properly. If we accept the grace He gives and the measure of faith He gives, we will consider ourselves and others the way we should. Paul alludes back to 12:1-2, so the reason-able act of worship means we have the grace and faith to love others with a sound mind. With 12:1-3 setting the tone of the two greatest commandments, let's see how Paul continues to teach about the second of those two commandments.

Read Roman 12:9-13:7. Use the table to list what Christians are to do and not do.

Verse	To Do/Not to Do

How does obeying these verses fulfill loving one's neighbor as oneself?

Notice Romans 12:16. Of what verse in Philippians 2 does this remind you?

What does it say about our minds?

Write what the passages below say about loving our neighbors:

James 2:8-19:

James 3:13-18:

James 4:11-12; 5:7-9:

Matthew 5-7:

Romans 13:8-10:

Romans 13:8-10 involves some Jewish history. How the Jews and rabbis interpreted the OT is important for our understanding of these verses. Jesus used the OT and Jewish literature of the Second Temple Period (530 BC-70 AD) when He taught about love. Since Christianity came from Judaism and Jewish leaders interpreted the Hebrew Scriptures, those teachings help us interpret these verses.

Do you think that Romans 13:9 teaches inappropriate self-love?   Why or why not?

How would such self-love contrast with 12:3?

Scriptural love of self is not narcissistic. God's command requires love for our neighbor over ourself. However, we must have a healthy self-worth. Rather than catering only to self—looking only to our own needs—we have to see ourselves as God see us in order to love others as God sees them.

How does your own self-worth define your love for others?

Read Ephesians 1. List the positive statements God says about you.

Where do you get your self-worth?

In Romans 13:9, Paul quotes Leviticus 19:18b: *you shall love your neighbor as yourself*. He says any commandment is summed up by this saying. Leviticus 19:1-20:27 explains and expands the Decalogue in how the Israelites should deal with fellow Jews and foreigners.[91] God commands the Israelites to love through their attitudes and actions toward others.

God knows people cannot love this way without His love in them. He expects obedience through love for Him. In Leviticus 19:18, the command indicates *loving a fellow Israelite*,[92] but in 19:34 God uses the same terminology for *the stranger* living among His people.

In this passage God demands the Israelites treat the stranger as if that person were *a native*. The word for *native* is *someone with the same worth*. The Jews should remember their status in Egypt and the harsh treatment they received there. They should realize that any human being needs to receive the value and love God gives.

This passage has a subtle missionary message. The Israelites should extend the love of God to other nations. Their holy devotion to God should shine through their behavior to insiders and outsiders. They should teach others why Yahweh God is the true God who loves all people.

---

[91]   Jeffrey M. Cohen, "Love of Neighbor and its Antecedent Verses," *JBQ* 24, no. 1 (January-March 1996): 19.

[92]   John E. Hartley, *Leviticus*, WBC 4, ed. David A. Hubbard and John D. W. Watts (Dallas: Word Books, 1992), 305, 309, 318.

As the Lord Jesus reflects on the Decalogue, He takes the implication of loving neighbors in other nations even further. With the first table of the Decalogue summarized in the first great commandment, and the second table grouped under the second great commandment, the Lord shows He expects even greater obedience. Love is the basis for *whatever* the Lord commands.

What do you need to change in your view of yourself so you can love others well?

Our excursus on obedience has involved both the Double Love Command and the Decalogue. Because both Paul and Jesus refer to the commandments, let's examine what the Ten Commandments say about loving others. We will look at the six commandments that deal with interpersonal relationships.

The Decalogue in Relation to Loving Others

Read the following passages. Complete the chart by writing the commands as stated in the OT verses. Then compare the OT and NT for each command. Answer how each one applies to love.

Commands	Exodus 20: 8-17	Leviticus 19:1-37	Deuter-onomy 5:12-21	How do the OT passages differ?	How they are similar?	Compare these NT passages with the OT verses on how to love your neighbor:
Parents						Romans 1:28-32: 2 Timothy 3:1-5: Mark 7:9-13: Ephesians 6:1-4: Colossians 3:20-21:
Killing						Matthew 5:21-22:

Stealing						Romans 2:21 (Consider ways you might steal.): Ephesians 4:28:
False Witness						Mark 14:55-58: Romans 1:29: 1 Timothy 5:19:
Coveting						Romans 7:7-12: Ephesians 5:1-5:
Adultery						Matthew 5:27-32: Galatians 5:19-21: Jas 2:11-13:

The Command with a Promise

Which command carries a promise?

What does that promise mean for you?

Do you have a problem with this commandment?   Why or why not?

Some people struggle loving and honoring parents who are harsh or abusive. We do not have to love what people do, but we do have to love *them*. We do not honor our parents or anyone else if we let them continue the abuse. We do not love ourselves as God loves us. When we allow abuse to continue, we *enable* those people to disobey God about how they are to love. We need to get godly help to handle the abuse and learn that we do not deserve that kind of treatment.

The Command Foundational to the Others

Read Romans 7:7-12 and Ephesians 5:5. How does the command against coveting differ from the other nine?

Read Genesis 4:1-8. What correlation do you see between coveting and the other commandments?

Why would Paul point to coveting in Romans 7:7-12 to teach him about the Law?

Read Mark 7:1-24. What do you see as the correlation of attitude and action?

How do Mark 7:1-24 and Philippians 2:1-13 relate to each other?

The Commands and the Golden Rule

In Romans 13:10, Paul exhorts the readers that love *does no wrong* to a neighbor. In 13:10a, Paul states the antithesis of 13:9b. When we love our neighbors as ourselves, we cannot wrong a neighbor. Leviticus 19:18a introduces 19:18b with the "Jewish Golden Rule," stating, "That which you hate do not do to your fellows; this is the whole law."[93] Some Jewish leaders reverse the order of Leviticus 19:18: "You shall love your neighbor, so that what is hateful to you,

---

[93]   Dunn, *Romans 9-16*, 778.

you shall not do to him."[94] Either way, this verse forms the greatest authority of the law: love does not violate any other commandments.[95]

Jesus restates Leviticus 19:18a or the Golden Rule in a positive direction (Matt 7:12 and Lk 6:31): "Do unto others what you would have them do unto you." Jesus says that whatever a person does in love fulfills the whole law. Paul says love does not demand vengeance, but expects us to consider others the way we hope to be treated.[96]

Reflect on the study of loving the Lord and others. List what has impacted your life and how you have changed because of those teachings.

Now let's return to Philippians 2:12-13. Keep love for God and others in mind as we hear Paul teach more about joy, unity, and obedience.

Philippians 2:12-13. How does verse 2:13 help your understanding of verse 12 and being obedient?

Obedience at All Times

In Philippians 2:12 we have already discussed that Paul tells the people to obey at all times. Paul reminds the Philippians of the positive choice they made to obey God when they first believed. They need to continue with the same passion and action *for God* despite who is watching.[97]

Obedience, when no one sees us, demonstrates our integrity—our determination to stand firm. The phrase *work out your salvation* does not imply works *for* salvation. Paul would be contradicting himself later in the letter.

How does Paul explain Philippians 2:12 in 2:13?

---

94 Keith D. Stanglin, "The Historical Connection between the Golden Rule and the Second Greatest Command," *JRE* 33, no. 2 (June 2005): 360-1.

95 J. P. McBeth, *Exegetical and Practical Commentary on the Epistle to the Romans* (New York: Fleming H. Revell Company, 1937), 238.

96 In both passages, Jesus said: *in everything, therefore, as much as you want people to do to you, in this way also you do unto them*. In Matthew, Jesus adds *for this is the Law and the Prophets*.

97 Hawthorne, *Philippians*, 98.

From Philippians 2:13, list the prepositions and how they are used.

Literally, verse 13 says: "For God is the one working *in* you both with the result that *the will* and *the work* are for the sake of His *desire*" (italics mine). The use of *in* implies the *close association within a limit*. God *wills* to live and work within our limited physical bodies.[98]

Why do you think God would do this?

The infinitives *to will* and *to work* indicate what *God* is doing in us and *through* us. Paul is using another play on words. He tells us to "'work out' what God 'works in.'"[99] God wills and works according to what *He* wants. The word for *desire* can mean *good will, pleasure,* or *purpose.* What God does, brings Him the glory He deserves.

Does it seem like God possesses an inappropriate self-love, even though He does not want us to be narcissistic?

Do you feel inappropriately used?

God cannot sin. He requires love and work for His glory so the world sees what a loving, trustworthy God He is. God cannot contradict what He expects from us. The work of the Spirit *through us* brings God the honor He deserves because He is *God*. We should never see God as inappropriately desiring our love.

When God uses us to work for Him, we really have the privilege of being in the company of Almighty God as *He* works. God's pleasure is to work together *with us* for His glory. He never uses us improperly. He lets us be a part of what He does. We are in an honored position! That is why we said in the section on Philippians 2:3 that we can give the Lord the glory for what He allows us to do—He has given us the ability and He has done the work through us.

What are the benefits of God's working through us?

How do you feel about that?

In 2:13 the apostle uses the same Greek word, *energéo*, both for *work* and *do*. We get our word *energy* from that Greek word. The literal meaning is *to work mightily, to work efficiently.*

---

98   *BDAG,* s. v. θέλω.
99   Melick, *Philippians, Colossians, Philemon,* 111.

We can see God giving us the energy to love Him with all our strength and to stand firm in obedience.

Read 1 Corinthians 15:38, 2 Corinthians 5:2, and Romans 8:9-11. In each passage tell what work is done and who does the work:[100]

1 Corinthians 15:38:
2 Corinthians 5:2:
Romans 8:9-11:

Working in our own strength and for our own glory is not what He wills. We can try to do whatever the Lord commands, but we will never *effectively* work in our own power. Our efforts in our strength do not bring Him pleasure. We possess the resurrection power of the Holy Spirit. This *same power* from the *same will* of the *same God* through the *same Spirit* raised Christ from the dead. He is pleased when we let *Him* work His power through us.

Now how do you feel about what you just read?

Living in the Light of Life

Philippians 2:14-16. Notice the wording of 2:14. Compare 2:12 with this verse about how we are to work out our salvation:

With _____ and _____, not with _____
or _____.

How does the last part of verse 13 relate with verse 14?

Evaluate 2:14-16 in light of 2:1-5. What are the reasons we are not to grumble and argue?

How do verses 2:14-16 align with the concept of unity?

How do grumbling and disputing affect our witness?

---

[100] Fee, *Pauline Christology*, 404.

Reread Philippians 1:3-4. When we are grumbling, how does that affect the way we pray for others?

Verses 1:5-6 tell us how to pray, (even when we want to gripe about a person). What are the two reasons?

1.
2.

Verse 1:7d gives another reason we should not grumble. Write that reason here.

What does Paul say in verse 1:8 about praying for others?[101]

Write what attitudes you discern in the following verses:

1:3-8:
2:5-11:
2:17-18:
2:14-16:

What do you think Paul is saying about his circumstance and that of Christ's?

Associate Paul's attitude with Christ's. Read 2 Timothy 4:6. What does Paul say about his life?

Philippians 2:17-18. Paul demonstrates his mindset when he compares his life to a drink offering. His life *possibly* is about to be poured out.

Investigate what Paul means by a drink offering. Read Numbers 15:1-26. Under the headings below, describe the drink offering and how it applies to other offerings. What size fits which offering?

        Numbers Passage   **Drink Offering**[102]

---

[101] Calvin Pearson, "Philippians 1," a taped sermon at SWBTS chapel, http://www.swbts.edu/events/chapel_archive.cfm (Fort Worth: SWBTS chapel, 28 October 2008; accessed 01 November 2008). Used by permission from Calvin Pearson and SWBTS.

[102] A *hin* is over six liters but not quite a gallon. The measurement actually varies by substance.

As a side note: why was the last offering given?

What sin had the Israelites committed?

How does that apply to us?

The drink offering accompanied other sacrifices or offerings, even the grain offering. Unlike the burnt sacrifice, the priest did not partake of this offering.[103] Possibly the priests did not drink the wine because of the command of the Lord in Leviticus 10:10. Priests were to avoid "strong drink because they were 'to distinguish between the holy and the common, and between the unclean and the clean.'"[104]

The drink offering was poured on the altar or at the foot of it, either on top of the sacrifice or after the offering. Unlike the libations which the pagans offered—which used blood even in Paul's day, the people of God were to use "the blood of the grape."[105] Wine replaced blood for the libation.

Paul described his death as a drink offering. He saw his life as an offering he gladly would give. Of course Paul did not die for the sins of people.

When Christ became obedient to death, He offered His blood for sin because without the spilled blood no remission for sin could be accepted. Christ's blood became the libation. He described His sacrifice differently.

> Read Matthew 26:26-29, Mark 14:22-25, and Luke 22:14-20. How does Christ describe the drink?

What do these passages say about the blood of Christ?

How do the Gospels differ?

What do we learn from each Gospel passage?

What promises do we as believers have concerning this drink?

---

[103] Thomas D. Lea and Hayne P. Griffin, Jr., *1, 2 Timothy, and Titus*, NAC 34, ed. David S. Dockery et al (Nashville: Broadman Press, 1992), 247n69.

[104] J. Julius Scott, Jr., *Jewish Backgrounds of the New Testament* (Grand Rapids: Baker Books, 1995), 254.

[105] Hawthorne, *Philippians*, 105.

Read Exodus 24:8. How does this passage explain the covenant of those NT passages?

Read Jeremiah 31:31-34 and Ezekiel 16:59-60. What do these verses say about a different covenant?[106]

What correlation do you see in Jeremiah 31:34 and Luke 22:14-20?

In Mark 14:25, Jesus says He will no longer drink the cup until the He drinks it new in the kingdom of heaven. Some of us may think He meant that He and the disciples were about to finish the meal, or that this was the only cup of juice the people drank at the meal.[107] The Passover meal, however, has four cups of wine which represent the four points of God's promise of redemption.

Read Exodus 6:6-7. Beside each number below, list the four promises God makes to His people in Egypt:

1.
2.
3.
4.

The four cups represent that God would *rescue* them from Egypt, *rid* them of their bondage, *redeem* them from their slavery, and *restore* the covenant He made with Abraham, Isaac, and Jacob.[108] The Lord stopped at the cup which stood for "I will redeem you." Jesus fasted from this cup. He would not commemorate the Passover Lamb. He would *be* the Passover Lamb who would redeem mankind.[109]

This picture also provides the assurance of His *parousia* or second coming. The image reminds us that as His people, we will drink the cup with Him in heaven. Jesus gave this promise before His death and resurrection, so His disciples could rest assured that death is not final.[110]

This cup means that Christ's blood would be poured out. The cup demonstrates the violent death He would die. The drink offering would accompany the grain or bread offering in the OT. Christ has offered His body as the bread, but His blood is the blood of the sacrifice for sin. Therefore, Jesus combines the images to show His death and shed blood were sufficient.

Breaking the bread demonstrates two things:

---

[106] Throughout the OT and NT, God bases His covenants on love, so in reality they are not much different in most of the characteristics; Joel B. Green, *The Gospel of Luke*, NICNT, ed. Ned B. Stonehouse, F. F. Bruce, and Gordon D. Fee (Grand Rapids: William B. Eerdmans,, 1997), 761.

[107] William L. Lane, *The Gospel according to Mark*, NICNT, ed. Ned B. Stonehouse, F. F. Bruce, and Gordon D. Fee (Grand Rapids: William Eerdmans Publishing, 1974), 508; Green, *The Gospel of Luke*, 761.

[108] Lane, *The Gospel according to Mark*, 507-509; Green, *The Gospel of Luke*, 761.

[109] Lane, 508.

[110] Ibid., 508.

First, as Christ broke the bread in the feeding of the five thousand (Luke 9; John 6) and the four thousand, He would break His own body to feed and redeem others spiritually.

Second, the bread illustrates distribution. Jesus would allow the breaking of His body in death for everyone. As the Lord distributed the bread in feeding the crowds and at the Passover meal, He alone could allocate His body to provide salvation for all.[111] Still, people have to accept Jesus' sacrifice to cover their sins.

Jesus instituted the Lord's Supper, or the Eucharist (Communion) right before His death. We, His followers, are to celebrate the breaking of bread and drinking of the cup as a regular reminder of His death until He comes again. As we partake of the Supper, we need to recall how the Lord fulfilled the *entire sacrifice* for sin permanently—the animal, the grain, and the drink offerings.

As for Paul's drink offering, even though Paul certainly would not pay the price for sins, his death is not insignificant. Paul's attitude in his willingness to *die* for Christ comes from dying daily to his own desires. He would not want his will to get in the way of God's. He would die daily in order to *live* for Christ (Phil 1:21).

God does call some people to martyrdom. Not everyone has the call to die physically as a martyr for Christ. The word for *witness* in the Greek is μάρτυς (*martus*) which gives us the word for martyr. We do have the call to take up Christ's cross and die to self, daily. Remember we do this as a witness, *martus*, for Him (Luke 9:23-26; Acts 1:8).

My husband and I had a friend who lived such a life in another country. Daily he would go into the forests to witness for Christ, even when he knew his life could be in danger. Political and religious insurgents easily could have killed him at any time. Ironically, he died in an insurgent's bombing at a public place everyone thought was safe. Our friend was a martyr because of rebels, but in reality he had been a practicing martyr for Christ every day.

Read 2 Corinthians 4:1-12. Focus on 4:10-12. What does Paul contrast in each verse?

Why do we live constantly delivering ourselves to death?

What is the ultimate purpose of dying to self?

Read Hebrews 12:1-2. What attitude about dying did Christ have?

As I am thinking about offering sacrifices to the Lord, I am reminded about one of our grandsons when he was two-and-a-half years old. He was about to go into a "big-boy" bed. He needed to transition from his crib. He registered a little fear, but Benny lay down with him and rubbed his back. Our grandson took his usual long nap.

---

[111] See Green, *The Gospel of Luke*, 761-64.

When he awoke, I went into the room and praised him for taking a good nap. He chattered about being a big boy and doing a good job. The next day when it was time to take his nap, he asked his PePaw if he could sleep on the big-boy bed again. I cannot help but wonder if praising our little grandboy helped his willingness to work with us.

The Lord appreciates our praise. They are a sacrifice to Him. He is not childish in this delight. We do not praise God to "get Him to work with us," but the sacrifice of our lips *is* a sweet aroma to God. He is *worthy* of our continuous praise for who He is and what He does.

I have not always praised continuously. Too often I prefer to focus on the negative of what happens. Little things can really bother me. Coming from a harmful past, I anticipate what someone might do or say to hurt me, so I have an answer ready to protect myself. What a waste of time worrying about "What if's!" What a waste of joy! Praise is precious for developing the right attitude and dispelling fear.

I have wanted to change, and the Lord has been working with me. The most vivid experience of praising has been during the time I have been writing this study. I found a lump and went for a diagnostic test. I asked friends to pray.

After the test, I was called for a diagnostic ultra sound. As I lay attached to the machine and waited for the doctor, I chose to lie there and praise the Lord for whatever might come, for who He is, for what He could accomplish, for how He could care for me and others around me.

When the tests were read, no new lump existed! What is more, two lumps which I had carried for six years in the lymph nodes under my left arm had reduced in size. I was praising and thanking the Lord all the way home!

I do not want to praise the Lord only when great things happen. I want to bless the name of the Lord in all things. I still have to work at it, but the praise has been much more spontaneous and more often. What a difference praise makes in our attitudes about big *and* little things.

In Philippians 2:17-18, in a way, Paul practiced a "what-if"—what if he were to die. However, his attitude did not reflect worry, anger, or despair. He rejoiced and shared his joy. He encouraged the Philippians to rejoice with him that he could suffer for Christ.

Living as Godly Examples

Godly Exemplars

Philippians 2:19-30. Name the circumstance.

What were Paul's concern and attitude?

From verse 19, name how Paul acquired his attitude.

How could Paul have this hope when he says not many other people had a kindred spirit?

Read 2:22. How was Timothy different from other people Paul knew?

Read 2:23-24. What other hope did Paul have that kept him positive?

Paul knew that only a few people around him cared about the things of Christ. Paul did not find his hope in people, but in the Lord Jesus and the future work the Lord had for him to do. Paul **hoped** like this because he had total confidence—was totally persuaded—that the Lord would take care of details, big and small.

Read 2:23 and Hebrews 11:6. What word do they have in common?

The same Greek word appears in both passages. The context of both verses in Philippians and Hebrews indicates the same meaning. Paul had confidence because he recognized what the Lord had already done for him and Epaphroditus. Paul's friend had nearly died. In that experience we see Paul's and Epaphroditus' attitudes. They had hope.

Some people of Philippi were intent on seeking their own desires, but Timothy and Epaphroditus were different. The two men shared the kindred spirit of seeking the welfare of others. The verb for seeking is present tense, which denotes a constant action. Their kindred spirit came because they were united *as one soul having the same desire*, the way Paul wanted the whole Philippian church to be (1:27; 2:20; 4:2). The men thought alike as if they were the same person: equal souls with each other and with Paul.

Read Matthew 26:37 and Mark 14:33.[112] What do you see in these verses that is the same in Philippians 2:26?

The Greek word for distressed is the same in these passages. How distressed was Epaphroditus?

Why?

In Matthew 26, Jesus had the weight of the world on His shoulders. Epaphroditus carried a similar concern for other people. Paul's helper was troubled that the people in Philippi would worry about him. He was one of theirs. They had sent him to Paul as part of their ministry to the apostle.

---

[112] *BDAG*, s. v. ἀδημονέω.

In verses 26-30, we realize how Epaphroditus has put his whole life into what the Philippians sent him to do. Paul uses the term *psyche* to indicate the *life* of Epaphroditus (2:30). By choosing that word, Paul involves Epaphroditus' soul and mind. Epaphroditus' soul longs with its very life, and his mind focuses itself on the Philippians' concerns.[113]

Read Philippians 1:8, James 4:5, and 1 Peter 2:2. What kind of *longing* is this?

When was the last time you longed for someone in this way?

When was the last time you longed for someone to come to Christ so much that your whole mind, body, soul, and determination were involved?

From 2:27-28, write what Paul says about suffering through illness.

I firmly accept that God wants to bless His people greatly, and will. He wants to heal supernaturally and does. I have been the recipient of supernatural healings when all medical treatments did not work. I have received many material blessings I do not deserve. I tend to lean on the side of Scriptural interpretation that says we do not receive enough of God's blessings because we do not take God's Word seriously.

However, I also cannot tell people if they would have enough faith they would be healed, would not have problems, or would have more material goods. I feel believers will suffer in this life. As we see from Paul—a great man of faith—he was unable to heal Epaphroditus and illness was a part of suffering for both men. I accept that Philippians is one of the NT books which teaches growth through suffering, that we will suffer as servants of the Lord.

Reread 2:29. How did Epaphroditus risk his life?

Have you ever risked your life like that?

Are you willing to do so?

In this passage we see how Epaphroditus loves the Lord and others deeply. He has given of himself with all his heart, soul, mind, and strength. His compassion and concern provide a serious illustration of service.

We see Paul loving the Lord and others deeply. Even though Paul knows sending Timothy and Epaphroditus to Philippi would leave him without help, he has chosen to do what would

---

[113] Witherington, *The Paul Quest*, 211; *BDAG*, s. v. ψυχή.

bring others cause for rejoicing. He wants to relieve the concern on the hearts of people he loves.

What needs to change in us and the church for our attitudes to be like Paul's, Timothy's, Epaphroditus', and Christ's?

Philippians 3:1. What does Paul tell his readers to do?

Chapter Three

A Song in Minor Key

A Modulation from Joy to Woe (3:1)

Philippians 3:1. Why does Paul again tell his readers to rejoice?

Verse 3:1 is another transitional verse. Paul reminds his readers to rejoice like Timothy and Ephaphroditus. Paul believes praise and rejoicing can safeguard his readers.

Remember I said that right now the Lord is working on me to rejoice and to praise at all times. I do not make New Year's resolutions. I believe if the Lord is working in me, He will show me what needs to change and will direct the changes throughout the year. God works on each of us daily.

What do you want to see the Lord do in your life this year, so you have the attitude of Timothy and Ephaphroditus?

In light of Philippians 2:14-3:1, what things can hinder our spontaneous or deliberate praise?

What other things, not mentioned in Philippians, might hinder praise?

Name some people like Ephaphroditus who have touched your life. Beside each name, tell how that person ministered to you. Then spend time praising the Lord for each person.

The Song of Woe: The Need for Humility and Hope (3:2-16)

Resonating a Warning (Fortissimo)

Philippians 3:2. Contrast this verse with 2:29. What is different in 3:2?

Read 1 John 4:1. What are believers to do? (This takes us back to loving God with our minds.)

Like Paul says in Philippians 3:2 and John says in 1 John 4:1, who would be the "dogs, evil workers, false circumcision," or "false prophets" in today's church?

In the first century, the issues of Jesus as Son of man and Son of God—Jesus in human flesh and as divine—caused division in the church. False teachers who said they were Christians made salvation harder. They were adding things to the belief in Jesus Christ for salvation. Both Paul and John did not want to add confusion to salvation or to growth in relationship with Jesus.

In Paul's diatribe of Philippians 3, he speaks against the people who demand that Christians keep the law to *get in* or *stay in* relationship with God. These Judaizers are Christians who legalistically are clinging to circumcision, food laws, and feast and Sabbath days. Paul is not going against Judaism or Jewishness in general. We will see later that Paul speaks of his Jewish background, so he is not anti-Semitic.[1]

Two things in Paul's language of 3:1-3 need an explanation:

1. what Paul is saying;
2. how Paul is saying it.

Read Galatians 1:6-9. What does Paul say to anyone who adds to or subtracts from the gospel? (Jesus plus or Jesus minus)

Read Galatians 3:1-14. Is Paul angry with the Galatians?   Why or why not?

Read Galatians 5:11-12. Does Paul really mean what those verses say?

Read Titus 1:12-13. How kind do those words sound?

Along with Galatians 3:1-14, can we say Paul is angry with some people?

---

[1]   The Jews are not the only Semitic people. For sake of this study, anti-Semitic as it is used today will represent the Jewish people. See Brian J. Dodd, *The Problem with Paul* (Downers Grove: InterVarsity Press, 1996), 112-14.

Read Ephesians 4:25-27 and Galatians 6:1. Tell why the previous passages seem to contradict what Paul has said?

Why would Paul tell people to speak the truth in love and seem so harsh in other instances?

Paul is exercising both Hebraic and Hellenistic types of literary or rhetorical speech. However, he is angry with people who pervert the gospel and confuse others. He uses terms which *draw attention* to what he is saying. Paul calls people "dogs" because of what they do to the gospel.[2]

The term *dogs* implies impurity or profane faith. Neither the Jews nor the Gentiles liked dogs, but the Jews called the Gentiles "dogs" for not being Jews or not believing in YHWH. Here Paul is speaking particularly to the Jewish false teachers about their profane faith.

Read Acts 15:1-32. In 15:13-29, what instructions did James give for becoming Christians?

What instructions did he give for living the Christian life?

How does James 2:1 agree with Acts 15:13-29?

What do Acts 15:1-2 and 15:24 tell us about the false doctrine of Philippians 3:2?

From Acts 15:1, 7-11, what does Peter say about the Gentiles coming to faith?

Paul attended the Jerusalem Conference. He knew that James and the leaders of the church in Jerusalem did not agree with the false teachers. Paul knew that James did not believe in works for salvation (Read Gal 1:18-19).

Philippians 3:2-3. Explain the false circumcision group.

---

[2]   The interpretation is mine. For an interesting essay which explains Paul's rhetoric, see Lauri Thuren, "Was Paul Angry?: Derhetorizing Galatians," in *The Rhetorical Interpretation of Scripture: Essays from the 1996 Malibu Conference*, eds. Stanley E. Porter and Dennis L. Stamps, JSNTSup 180, ed. Stanley E. Porter (Sheffield: Sheffield Academic Press, 1999), 302-30.

Read Romans 2:28-29 and Philippians 3:2-3. How does the false circumcision differ from true circumcision?

In the English translation, we do not realize the impact of the term *false circumcision*. Paul uses another word play to contrast the two groups. The Greek for false circumcision is a word that means "mutilation, cutting in pieces . . . probably to denote those for whom circumcision results in (spiritual) destruction."[3]

The false teachers claim that God requires circumcision as the Christian's mark of salvation. In other words, some Judaizers taught that people had to become Jews to become Christians. Paul was warning the Philippians to be on their guard against such erroneous views. As the servant of the Lord and apostle of the gospel, Paul had the authority to speak against such "profanity." In so doing, Paul spoke against the teaching which made the Judaizers proud of their Jewish separateness in circumcision, food, and festival laws.

Paul's pun says: "You mutilated ones, you who are 'cut to pieces' rather than 'cut around,' we are the circumcised in heart. Our hearts have been cut around where Christ cut away our sin, but our hearts are still intact. We are still whole."[4]

Physical circumcision was a *sign* of spiritual circumcision in the OT. God never intended for this to be the deed for salvation or justification. Abraham believed God and was credited with righteousness *before* the sign of circumcision came from God (Gen 15:6; 17:10-11).

Circumcision of the heart already had happened in Abraham; the physical sign came afterward. The Judaizers mistook the change of the body for the change of the heart. They rearranged the timeline and made the sign of obedience necessary for faith. The Judaizers misunderstood what Moses, Jeremiah, and the Lord had said: that God would circumcise their *hearts* to make them righteous (Deut 30:6-8).

In Philippians 3:3, what three things does the true circumcision group perform?

1.
2.
3.

In 3:2-3 we see the contrast between the three warnings and the three acts of true circumcision. Complete the table:

Three Warnings	Three Acts
1.	1.
2.	2.
3.	3.

---

3   *BDAG*: s. v. κατατομή.
4   Fee, *God's Empowering Presence*, 752

The word translated *worship* in the English fits better with the definition:"the offering of service to God in devotion."[5] Paul still plays on the concept of circumcision. The physical circumcision is an act of devotion for each Jewish male, but the false teachers have made it ritualistic and idolatrous.

Rather than being confident in the flesh, the true believers must boast in Christ. The false circumcision group could not serve God when insisting on the flesh or dragging others into such rituals. The true circumcision group should realize their life and service through the Spirit. The true believers would live vibrantly in the present in Christ; the false teachers would cling legalistically to the past.[6]

To what traditions are you clinging that hinder true faith and do not allow your faith to grow properly?

Philippians 3:4-6. Paul says not to put confidence in the flesh. Then he delineates why he can. List all the things about which Paul could boast in the same way as the Judaizers.

Paul uses himself as an example of someone who could boast in outward signs. He has done everything well according to the Law. Even though the Judaizers have tried to dismiss Paul as a false teacher, he shows the Philippians that he is someone who could stand alongside the Judaizers in fulfilling the law.

Read the passages below. Beside each Scripture passage, tell what the verses say about the law.

Matthew 19:16-21:

Acts 15:10-11:

Romans 2:17-24:

Romans 3:9-20:

---

[5]   Ibid.

[6]   Fee, *God's Empowering Presence*, 752.

Galatians 1:11-15:

Galatians 3:10-14:

Reread Philippians 3:6. How can Paul say he was blameless according to "the righteousness of the law"?

Paul was showing the Judaizers that even though he had the same pedigree or had an even better one than they, he could not expect it to earn salvation or keep it. Paul was addressing confusion in the church about how to be saved and how secure that salvation is. Let's look at the issue of securing and security in our salvation.

Read John 10:27-28. What does this say about how we have eternal life (salvation)?

Now read John 10:29. What does this say about our security in relationship with the Lord?

Read John 10:30. What assurance does this give you?

Read Romans 8:31, 37. What do these two verses say about security?

Read Ephesians 1:13-14, 18-23 and 1 Peter 1:3-9. List as many ways as you can see in these verses that tell how we know we are secure in Christ?

Read Ephesians 2:4-10. How can we be *sure* we are secure? (Hint: Where do we sit right now?)

In all these passages, what does God do?

What do we do? (Return to 1 Peter 1:6-8 for a BIG hint.)

The idea of a gift may have a different connotation in today's world. I remember growing up that even if we did not like a gift, we kept it. We may have stuffed it in a closet or an attic. We may have pulled it from the closet or attic when the giver was at the house, but we kept it. Today we re-gift or return the gift if we do not like it.

Concerning salvation, grace, or faith, God's gift is a permanent fixture in our lives. We accept the gift, but we are not to stuff it in the closet of our hearts or the attic of our minds. Plus, we need to understand exactly what the *gift* is. In Ephesians 2:4-10, we see that the gift is the *process* of salvation by grace through faith—all of that, Christ gives.

Let's focus on the wording in Ephesians 2:8-9. Write those verses here.

The Greek words for faith and grace are feminine nouns. That emphasis is important, because in the Greek any modifier—adjective or article (a, an, the)—of faith or grace will need to be feminine. The word *that* is neuter. A literal translation of Ephesians 2:8 is

For by grace you have been saved through faith and that a gift of God not of yourselves.

That refers to the phrase of having been saved by grace through faith. The phrase implies the process of salvation. Verse 9 says the gift is not because of our works or we would have reason to boast about our achieving our salvation.

Instead, we do not do the earning; God does the giving and God gives the process from start to finish! First Peter 1:3 says *God has caused* us to be born again. In Ephesians 1:18-23 and 1 Peter 1:3-4 we have the living hope of a promised inheritance, and God does the keeping in heaven where we *already* sit with Christ. We will be tempted to sin, because we are not perfect yet—we are still being perfected.

We will endure testing and trials. In 1 Peter 1:7, we see that the trials test our faith to prove it. To prove is the same idea in Psalm 139:23. The proof is the action that melts off the dross. Testing is not to disconnect us from the Lord, but bring us closer to Him. Peter compares our faith with gold that is imperishable, so he teaches that our faith does not perish.

We know from what Paul says that the Lord takes us through the trials. *His Spirit* carries us through—we have studied Romans 5:3-5 several times and see hope for our continued salvation. Our salvation does not fail.

We also know that the Spirit gives us work to do after our initial salvation experience. Those works do not get us into salvation. They do not keep us in salvation. Remember, the works demonstrate our love for the Lord through our worship and love for others.

Scripture does indicate that our works *after* salvation will be judged, but God's Word specifically says that only through grace can people come into relationship with Jesus Christ. Only through grace do people stay in relationship. The Holy Spirit seals and keeps each person in relationship with Jesus. The Holy Spirit works within each person so no one can boast about the work that is done to get in or stay in.

An evangelist once held a revival in a church Benny pastored. During a lunch meeting, the preacher used the illustration of eternal security that has stayed with me vividly. He quoted the verses we just learned from John and Ephesians. Here is the gist of the illustration.

Take a coin; put it in your right hand and close your hand tightly. Next have someone else put both of his or her hands over yours. Your hand represents the Son's hand. The other two represent the Father's and Spirit's hands. Now have a third person try to take the coin from *your* right hand. How easy would that be?

Consider three very important facts about this kind of security:

First, Jesus—as God—has *given* the eternal life. No one can pluck us out of His hands—not even us. Once we have salvation, the Lord keeps the salvation. If we cannot earn salvation, we cannot un-earn it. We can choose to live as a good witness in a close relationship—and we should, for our love reflects being *in Christ*.

Second, we are in the Father's hands. Certainly no one can pluck us out of the hands of the All-Powerful God! In 1 Peter 1:4-5 we see that we receive an inheritance which is imperishable, undefiled, and will not fade. It is reserved in heaven for us, *protected by the power of God*. Even though the inheritance comes through faith, God is protecting the fully-completed salvation and will reveal it later.

Third, we are *sealed* by the Holy Spirit of promise. The Greek word for sealed in Ephesians 1:13 means "the concept of sealing *eschatologically*"[7] (italics are mine). That verse means the Holy Spirit comes into our lives the moment we accept Jesus as our Savior. The Spirit *certifies*,[8] "This one is saved eternally." The word *promise* means that God has *obligated Himself* to carry out what He says He will do.[9] Philippians 1:6 assures us of that very fact. Therefore since God has said no one can pluck us from His hand, He will fulfill that promise into eternity.

Another important feature is the form of the Greek verb which Paul uses in Ephesians 1:13. Three things are very significant about that verb:

First, the verb is *aorist tense*. That means: the deed covers the whole achievement from start to finish.[10] It is a done deal! While we have not seen the end result, in God's eyes our salvation is finished for all eternity.

Second, the verb is *passive voice*. The Holy Spirit does the action *to* us. We do not have anything to do with whether we are secure. He does the sealing. He puts that stamp on our lives: *sealed for eternity*. That means we cannot seal or unseal ourselves. No one else can unseal us.

---

7   *BDAG*, s. v. σφραγίζω.

8   Warren C. Trenchard, *Complete Vocabulary Guide to the Greek New Testament*, rev. ed. (Grand Rapids: Zondervan, 1998), s. v. σφραγίζω, 106.

9   *BDAG*, s. v. ἐπαγγελία.

10 Daniel B. Wallace, *Greek Grammar: Beyond the Basics: An Exegetical Syntax of the New Testament* (Grand Rapids: Zondervan, 1996), 557.

Third, the aorist is a *constative aorist.* That big term means we can *know* the sealing is *true*, is *complete.* We do not have to wonder *if* we are sealed. The *verb form* stresses the **fact** that we are sealed eternally.[11] With God's Spirit doing the sealing, how could we not be secure? We can be *sure* the Spirit has sealed us because *God says* He has.

Ephesians 1:14 says the Lord has given the Spirit as a pledge. The Spirit pledges our inheritance that we are redeemed, that we are God's own possession. The idea of a seal in the first century indicates that God has *complete legal ownership* and we are stamped with: **Belongs to God**.

Just as that coin belongs to us and we have no intention of losing it, we can be sure that Father God through Jesus the Son holds us as His possession all the way into heaven. If it would be hard for someone to take that coin from our hands or even for us to lose that coin with three hands around it, think how hard it would be for anything or anyone—even us—to remove us from the hand of Jesus when He, the Father, and the Holy Spirit own us and have us in Their grasp.

To me, that is security that will last until I see Jesus face to face. There, we finally will *see* the finished product of our lives. Plus, we have the Spirit living in us now as the *personal guarantee* from God.

Read Numbers 23:19, Romans 3:4, 2 Timothy 2:13, Titus 1:2, and Hebrews 6:18. What do these verses tell us about God, and therefore His promise to seal us?

How does this illustration of security help you and make you feel?

It makes me *feel* as Peter says: *full of joy inexpressible and full of glory for God.* I want to *do* what Peter says: **shout Hallelujah!! Glory to God!!!!**

Praise the Lord with me. Praise the Lord for your security, and assurance of that security. Show your zealous feelings about how delighted you are that God has saved you and is keeping you!

The problem with the zealousness of the Judaizers in Philippi was their insistence that their obedience to the Law had *earned* their salvation. They felt they knew better than Paul how to be in a relationship with God. They boasted that they were better Jews and Christians than Paul. The Judaizers claimed they could *stay* in their relationship with Christ only through obedience to God's commands. As Jewish Christians, they clung to the past and boasted about *their* efforts.

---

[11]   Wallace, *Greek Grammar*, 557.

Read Jeremiah 9:23-24. What do these verses say about boasting?

Paul most likely echoes the Jeremiah passage. He recognizes that even though he could boast about his Jewish heritage, he has something better about which to boast. Paul uses these verses to set the stage for the next verse of his lifesong.

Philippians 3:7. What does Paul feel about his former pedigree?

How are we to consider such honors in our lives?

When we lived in South Korea, I could have thought I had a pedigree, if someone wants to call it that. As a missionary, pastor's wife, mathematics teacher, and English teacher, I received honor from the Korean people; they showed me they valued me for those positions. They paid high respect to *Somonim*, which means "the wife of someone important" or "a woman of importance." The last syllable in Somonim is an honorific suffix. Added to any title, *nim* means the person deserves respect.

I returned from the mission field to no position whatsoever. Because of my husband's health, we could not go back to Korea or anywhere else. I did have two statuses—student and pew warmer. Oh, I already knew if we find our value in our accomplishments and titles, we can lose the status and suddenly feel tremendously worthless. I had to work through the grief of the loss of those positions. I could keep the memories, but I did not need to get my value from them.

On the other hand, I still can wear several titles: Christian, beloved of God, pray-er, wife, mother, grandmother, and daughter. All of them carry respect. They are all very important and they represent key roles in my life.

Paul realizes that in spite of the religious and ethnic Jewish ladder he had been climbing, he was nothing without Jesus Christ. He sees those titles and accomplishments as a part of his past to put in the loss column.[12] In view of the value of knowing Christ—experientially—he has found that Christ outweighs everything.

Philippians 3:7-11. Where does Paul place those titles?

What other things does he put there?

The English translations of these verses are often too polite. Paul calls those things *excrement*. The KJV has it right when it translates the Greek word as *dung*. Those things were

---

12   Jerry L. Sumney, *Philippians: A Greek Student's Intermediate Reader* (Peabody, MA: Hendrickson Publishers, 2007), 77.

revolting to Paul, just like animal feces. Those things did not make Paul righteous and he does not want to cling to them.

Read Isaiah 64:6. What does the prophet Isaiah say about one's own righteousness?

Consider the filthiest, worst smelling, bloody rag imaginable. Write your description here.

Isaiah 64:4 is very graphic in the Hebrew. Our sins are as dirty to God as the *filthiest* bloody rag. To God, even our good deeds—*which we perform in our own strength*—are equal to those filthy rags; they are sin in God's eyes.[13]

The literal translation of the Hebrew, which I mention in the footnote, may not seem appropriate for me to put in a Bible study—especially if studied in a mixed-gender group—but sin is serious to God. He had Isaiah incorporate a word for *filthy* which is not used anywhere else in Scripture. When a word is used only once, it is called a *hapax legomenon*—a one-time word. Isaiah chose a *hapax legomenon* to describe just how filthy our sins, and so our own achievements, are in God's estimation. Possibly, the Judaizers' arrogance and aspirations of grasping onto a pedigree to prove their own righteousness reminded Paul of God's take on sin and fleshly deeds.

In Philippians 3:7-11, with what does Paul replace those trophies of his past? List them.

Compare 3:6 with 3:9. What does Paul tell us about his own righteousness?

Focus on 3:10-11. Again Paul replaces his pedigree with the new list. He considers sufferings and death as some things to be put in the *gain* column. Notice 3:10b and 3:11. To what does Paul refer in those verses?

How necessary are those things in order to attain what Paul desires in 3:10?

Paul uses an *inclusio* as a bracket for his concept. Paul has realized that suffering and dying with Christ offers more than anything in his past could. Knowledge of the Lord lasts

---

13   The literal translation is not usually used in English translations. The word "filthy" takes the place of *bloody menstrual rags*. God looks at our sins, and what we do in our own strength, with this graphic picture.

beyond this lifetime into eternity. Paul also knows that anything worth doing, any way worth *being*, must have the resurrection power of Christ.

Philippians 3:12. How does Paul realize his desire?

A story is told about a humble third-century Christian monk, Abba Agathon, who lived alone in the Egyptian desert. He had great discernment. Some fellow monks wanted to test how discerning and humble Agathon really was. They approached him in his room and asked if he were that Agathon who was said to be a sinner and a proud man. He said he was.

They asked another question. "Aren't you that Agathon who is always talking nonsense?" He answered that he was.

However on the third question, "Aren't you Agathon the heretic?" he immediately countered, "I am not a heretic."

When they wondered about his retort over the last insult, he replied that he could accept the first two accusations. Those would keep him humble. However, heresy would mean separation from God and he had "no wish to be separated from God."[14]

Paul would have understood Agathon's answer. When Paul says in Philippians 3:7-10 that he counts all things loss except to know Christ, he means he wants to know Christ in every way possible, as intimately as possible. Paul recognizes that to obtain this desire he has to continue with this mindset until the end of his life.

Such recognition is not a once-for-all moment where he will never sin or slip again. This desire is a daily pursuit of becoming mature and perfect, and teaching others the right principles. He could leave the past and press toward the finish line, because the prize—the goal—is his eternal life in heaven (Phil 3:13-16).

Philippians 3:12-16. Does Paul contradict his song of humility between 3:12 and 3:15?
Use a Bible concordance and commentary to research why or why not. You can find those online. Express the reasons here.

Write what the following verses add to the idea of perfection in 3:12-16:

Ephesians 3:17-19:

Ephesians 4:11-16:

Colossians 1:24-29:

---

[14]   *Orthodox Wiki*, http://orthodoxwiki.org/OrthodoxWiki:Copyrights (accessed 15 September 2011).

In Philippians 3:15-16, to what attitude does Paul refer?

What is the contrast which Paul mentions here?

Does Paul include himself in verses 15-16?

From 3:7-16, list things Paul says show his growth, his maturity in Christ.

Returning to verse 10, we see that Paul seeks *to know* something. That *something* is *Someone*. He desires the knowledge of only one object: Christ.

Paul contrasts the high to the low—from the power of Christ's resurrection to the fellowship of sufferings and death. Paul can know them all at the same time, but he has to realize the power first to achieve the other things properly. Paul is experiencing the tension of the "already-not yet" aspect of perfection.

He knows he is *already* complete or perfect in God's eyes, but has *not yet* finished maturing on earth. Paul has experienced sufferings and death daily for knowing Christ. He also understands he could only face them through the resurrection power of Christ's Spirit. Even though he could know Christ fully only after death, Paul is willing to do whatever is necessary daily to get closer to the Lord completely.

Remember that Ephesians 2:6, Colossians 1:27, and 3:1-3, 26 tell us we already sit in heaven. As we have discussed, the *already* of the resurrection and heaven is ours. However, because we have not reached full completion here and we are *not yet* what we should be, we still face sufferings and death on earth.[15] This *not-yet* fact applies to Paul's statement in verse 11. The better translation of verses 10-11 is that Paul *wants to know Christ in every way in order that he might arrive more completed at the resurrection from the dead*. Knowing Christ is the only way to experience resurrection or its power.

Read Romans 8:17. What does Paul indicate in this verse?

Paul knows that glorification, or the hope of resurrection to eternal life, does not happen without union with Christ first and that growth comes through sufferings second.[16] Paul recognizes that without the power of the resurrection, he cannot make it through suffering or death.

His primary goal is to know the person of Christ Jesus intimately through his sufferings and willingness to die. Paul uses a verb in Philippians 3:12 and an adjective in verse 15 which have the same root word for perfection. Paul contrasts the already perfect in 3:12 with the not-yet need to continue maturing in 3:15. Therefore, no contradiction exists from 3:12 to 3:15. Paul moves onward to be as mature and complete as he can.

Paul may have used this play on words as a contrast for any of several reasons:

---

[15]   Fee, *God's Empowering Presence*, 825, 837; Gal 2:20; Eph 2:6.
[16]   Silva, *Philippians*, 190-91.

First, the reference may point to those who think they are spiritually superior because they are

    a.   Jewish Christians;
    b.   observing the rites of Judaism;
    c.   from the mother church at Jerusalem.

These are "those dogs" (3:2), who believe they already have attained perfection.[17] They represent the attitudes against which Paul preaches in chapters 1-3 (Remember 1:15-30; 2:3-4; 3:2.).

Second, the contrast could imply that the Philippians do not fully understand the sanctification process. The people may have thought that coming to Christ at their initial point of salvation means they no longer have to worry about how they live.[18] They may be thinking they are perfect already.

Third, the seeming contradiction may come from the Philippians cowering from suffering (1:18-30). Paul could not force the Philippians to consider suffering as he did, but he could *encourage* them to have the same thoughts as he (2:1-5). The same noun for encourage in 3:15 is in 2:5.[19]

Fourth, Paul could have been using irony—tongue in cheek—to remind his readers that when they came to Christ, they still kept their human will. Human will diminishes through sufferings, so the image of Christ and His will achieve *completion*, from τέλιος, *telios*. Jesus used a form of this word right before He died when He said, "It is finished!" Jesus had completed our work of salvation. However, Paul knows that while Jesus has taken care of everything, everyone should have "the attitude that Christian perfection is in reality a *constant striving* for perfection."[20] Paul might command the people to change, but he cannot change their attitudes for them. He applies a softened approach here. He uses the verb form for "we should" or "let us."[21] Paul included himself in the admonition for growth in 3:15.

> Read Hebrews 12:1-3 and compare it with Philippians 3:10-14. Tell the way the writer of Hebrews says we have to win the prize.

> What does Hebrews 12:3 indicate is necessary to win the prize?

---

[17]   See Silva, *Philippians*, 205. Silva agrees that the context of chapter three could point to the Judaizers; Hawthorne disagrees.

[18]   Jac. J. Müller, *The Epistles of Paul to the Philippians and to Philemon*, NICNT (Grand Rapids: Wm. B. Eerdmans Publishing Company 1955), 126-27; Hawthorne, *Philippians*, 155.

[19]   Silva, *Philippians*, 206.

[20]   Hawthorne, *Philippians*, 156; the emphasis in italics is mine.

[21]   Ibid., 155-57.

Read Leviticus 19:2, Matthew 5:48, 2 Corinthians 7:1, and Hebrews 12:3-11. How do these verses relate to each other?

The writer of Hebrews was a close associate of Paul's. He could have heard Paul's letters read to the Corinthian church. He may also have known of Paul's prison letter to the Philippians. He would have known what Paul meant about being perfect. Both Matthew 5:48 and 2 Corinthians 7:1 use derivatives or forms of *telios* for maturity or completion.

In all these verses, how are *holiness* and *perfection* related?

Is all suffering caused by sin?

Does all suffering mean we are being punished or disciplined?

Read 1 Corinthians 9:24-27. What might be a difference in the meaning of punishment and discipline in the contexts of Hebrews 12:3-11 and 1 Corinthians 9:24-27?

The Greek words for *discipline* are different in those two passages. Hebrews 12 talks about discipline for instruction. First Corinthians 9:24-27 uses a word that means "to wear someone down," "to put under strict discipline, punish, treat roughly, torment."[22] This word goes with *telios*. Therefore, one pushes or "punishes" oneself very hard to complete the race.

While we must discipline ourselves for a race in order to win the prize, the discipline in Hebrews 12 is not a torment kind of punishment. Hebrews' discipline is one which trains, corrects, and educates. The Greek word comes from the word for child. Children have to learn discipline to become mature.[23]

Read Proverbs 3:1-12 and Hebrews 12:7-11. Beside each passage, list what these verses tell us about discipline and a proper attitude.

Proverbs 3:1-12:

Hebrews 12:7-11:

---

[22]   *BDAG*, s. v. ὑπωπιάζω.

[23]   F. F. Bruce, *The Epistle to the Hebrews*, NICNT, ed. F. F. Bruce (Grand Rapids: Wm. B. Eerdmans Publishing, 1964), 355-61; John MacArthur, Jr., *Hebrews*, The MacArthur New Testament Commentary (Chicago: Moody Publishers, 1983), 383-89.

We are to choose to press forward to reach the prize through the discipline which suffering causes. We still need to go through the sanctification process. Since suffering with Christ is part of growth, the development means God is teaching us to submit to His will, respect Him, obey Him, and be conformed to Christ's image. We become more like Christ as we endure trials *and* their disciplines.

A Brighter Song: Realizing Our New Citizenship (3:17-21)

Philippians 3:17. How does Paul's statement about imitation seem inconsistent?

Why would Paul tell the Philippians to imitate *him* if they are not to do anything for vain glory?

What is the pattern to which Paul is referring?

Investigate Philippians 3:2, 7, 12, 15, and 17. How does 3:17 fit with those other verses?

The noun for *example* in 3:17 is a compound word that Paul uses only here. He may have coined this *hapax legomenon* since the word does not appear in any other Greek literature.[24] The word literally means *a fellow-imitator*. The phrase indicates *keep on imitating me—together*.

Paul is emphasizing that he wants the whole group to follow his example, as some people already have been doing. The Philippians together should pursue the goal of knowing Christ as Paul wants to know Him. Paul uses verse 17 as a transition between 3:2-16 and 3:18-21. He exhorts his readers to emulate the people who live by the right standard. Since Paul knows the Philippians imitate other Christians—some obviously have been following the Judaizers and some have been following him—he wants the believers to be united in following his example.

Read 3:18-20. List the five things which make Paul weep and which comprise the pattern he does *not* want Christians to follow:

1.
2.
3.
4.
5.

---

24 Hawthorne, *Philippians*, 160.

From 3:7-21 describe the perspective and pattern Paul wants people to follow versus the pattern of the enemies:

Phil. 3:7-21	Paul's Pattern	The Enemy's Pattern
The Cross of Christ		
Whose End		
Whose God		
Whose Glory		
Whose Mindset		

Paul wants Christians to imitate him in the same way he imitates Christ. Paul has chosen to lower his own status as an apostle and be a tentmaker. Rather than expect the monetary benefits which the rank of an apostle could provide him, Paul has decided not to accept help from many benefactors. Often the benefits could come with strict expectations. Paul could have demanded the churches pay him or could have accepted the gifts from patrons. He usually did not do so because he did not want to tie himself to anyone who could require time away from the gospel. While he has accepted the Philippians' help, he tells us in 4:17 that he has allowed their help for their benefit and the benefit of others (See 2 Cor 9:1-5.). Paul knows that his actions not to grasp his rights as an apostle, imitate those of Christ.

Read Philippians 2:6-8 and 1 Corinthians 9:1-19. In the chart below, write the comparisons of Paul to Jesus.[25]

Philippians 2:6-8   **1 Corinthians 9:1-19**

---

[25] Gorman, *Apostle of the Crucified Lord*, 68-70, 260. The ideas come from Gorman. His comparison provides a vivid reason why Paul could expect his church members to imitate him as he imitates Jesus Christ.

Paul wants his readers to recognize something about their own mindset. He would prefer the Corinthians act like the Philippians. Both groups, and we today, can imitate Christ as Paul did.[26]

Read Philippians 3:20-21. What part of the enemies' mentality may the Philippians still have?

How could that affect them from keeping the pattern Paul wants them to imitate?

Remember that Philippi became a Roman colony in 42 B.C. A Roman colony meant the citizens of the city "did not pay taxes, tribute, and duties."[27] The people stood firm against anything that might spoil their protected status. When Claudius kicked Jews and Jewish Christians from Rome in A.D. 49—the year Paul probably arrived in Philippi—the Philippians took note of the trouble. The emperor's action deeply affected anything Christian citizens might try to do.

Read Acts 16:11-21. What was the real reason the girl's masters were upset?

What was the reason they gave the chief magistrates?

In light of Claudius' ruling, how would the second answer have affected the citizens of the city?

Read Acts 16:35 and Philippians 3:19-20. Based on what we have just discussed, what could be the underlying reason Paul would ask the Christians in Philippi not to *grasp* their earthly citizenship but yet Paul and Silas had clung onto theirs?

Paul knows living for Christ in Philippi could be hard. The new religion could bring persecution to the Christians. The believers, very proud of their relationship with Rome, might succumb to the government's demands to worship the Emperor rather than live for Christ. Paul has inserted political language throughout the letter, calling the Philippians to understand their citizenship in Christ's *new* community.

Remember Philippians 1:27. Paul uses an inclusio about conduct or citizenship there and citizenship in this section. Paul realizes the Philippians could lose their citizenship if they choose Christ. However, *clinging* to the physical government would mean releasing their connection to their new community. Just as they were willing to stand firm to keep their earthly,

---

[26]   See Gorman, *Apostle of the Crucified Lord*, 68-69.

[27]   M. Robert Mulholland, Jr., "Social Criticism," in *Interpreting the New Testament: Essays on Methods and Issues*, ed. David Alan Black and David S. Dockery (Nashville: Broadman & Holman Publishers, 2001), 180.

Roman citizenship, they would need to stand strong in the Christian community, in spite of what Rome might do to them.[28]

For Paul and Silas to appeal to their citizenship in Acts 16, they had to have a good reason. They needed to go to other cities and begin other churches. The men knew the Romans had beaten them and incarcerated them illegally, so they referred to their citizen rights in order to help others. They did not cling to what was not useful for the kingdom.

In Philippi, the enemies were using their rights only for themselves. In the letter Paul contrasts what the believers should do as Christians with what the opponents expect them to do. The enemies' end would be destruction (3:19).

Paul plays on the word *destruction*. The opponents' end means "literally, to be un-citied."[29] They would know the loss of what "gives meaning, value, identity, and purpose to the community and the individual."[30] Paul wants the Philippians to see that while their citizenship with Rome provides them great benefits, that empire will not last. In 3:20-21, Paul contrasts the lives of those who live as enemies of the cross of Christ with the believers. Those following Paul's pattern should agree to be a part of Christ's suffering and death.

Even if they were cast out by the government, Christians' end would be the life of Christ. If their earthly citizenship were gone, they still would have a heavenly one. They should seek to know Christ so they could know the power of His resurrection. Instead of seeking a glory of shame in disobeying God, they could have Christ's glory in a transformed body. They have a better place waiting for them. The believers should recognize that their suffering and their loss (3:7) come as part of God's purpose—His best.[31]

We today must recognize in suffering, we are imitators of Paul and of Christ for the sake of the gospel. We are witnesses of God's will and a "sign of belonging" to God's family.[32] The redemptive activity of God through Christ's suffering on our behalf and our suffering on behalf of the gospel is opposite our clinging to our citizenship here.[33]

As I was proofreading this study for publication, I learned of someone who was willing to give up his right and citizenship on earth because he embraced the cross. Some members of the ruling council of his country were trying to get religious freedom for their people. This leader said that he was thankful for the cross and was a follower of Christ. He said he was willing to die because he was a Christian. The next day, two radical groups opposed to his faith gunned him down. He chose to be more of a citizen of heaven than of an earthly country.

Read 1 Peter 4:12-19. What is the outlook Peter says we should have in suffering?

List the reasons we can take that outlook.

---

[28] The interpretation is mine. For illustration of the wide-spread emperor-cult practices, see Gorman, *Apostle of the Crucified Lord*, 16, 419.

[29] Mulholland, "Social Criticism," 182.

[30] Ibid.

[31] Donald Guthrie, *New Testament Theology* (Downers Grove, IL: Inter-Varsity Press, 1981), 97-98.

[32] Ibid., 97.

[33] Ibid., 98.

What should we avoid in our suffering?

Peter admonishes believers to have the same attitude which Paul has indicated in Philippians. Believers are to rejoice in suffering and do what is right. In Philippians 3:17-18, Paul says Christians should observe something about people who follow the right pattern as well as the people who don't. Paul uses the same verb for both the good and bad models. The difference is the outcome of the pattern each group chooses.

What is the verb in both 3:17 and 3:18?

Read Psalm 1:1a. How do Psalm 1:1a and Philippians 3:18 relate?

From Psalm 1:1, list the progression the enemies of the cross take.

People can choose to walk with or follow after the Spirit, or they can choose to walk with the enemies of the cross and embrace the counsel of the wicked.

When have you walked with the enemies of the cross?

As you remember that experience, how did you progress from walking with them, to standing in their path, to sitting in their council?

Describe how the Lord has brought you from that lifestyle to the pattern you follow now.

How do you stand firmly in harmony with other believers and sit in their council today?

In Chapter 4, we will see Paul continue to teach the right pattern to live. He develops his thoughts and gives us ways to experience the correct mindset. We definitely will experience more of his joy!

Chapter Four

A Call for Songs in Excellent Harmony

A Reminder to Stand Firm and Sing in Harmony (4:1)

Philippians 4:1. Where does Paul want the believers to stand?

Look again at Philippians 1:27, 3:17-4:1, and Psalm 1. Write the similarities you see in these passages.

Where does the walk end for the two different groups of people?

Possibly, Paul was considering this Psalm when he spoke of the enemies of the cross versus the believers. Psalm 1:3 and 6 tells *why* we should stand firm in the Lord. Write the reasons.

Psalm 1:2 tells *how* believers stand firm. What makes the difference between the enemies of the cross and those who walk according to the pattern (Phil 3:17)?

Is it possible for Christians to be enemies of the cross?

If so, what would allow or cause that to happen?

If not, why not?

Read Ephesians 4:30-32. What can we believers do that might make us appear as enemies of the cross?

Read 2 Corinthians 13:14, Ephesians 4:3-4, and Philippians 1:27-2:4. What do you notice about being in fellowship with the Spirit?

How does that happen?

Read Hebrews 3:6, 6:12, 10:23-24, and, 13:7. What else do we get when we imitate those who stand firm?

Read 1 Peter 1:5; 2:21; 4:1, 10, 19; and 5:1, 10. What examples help us hold fast?[1]

Read Isaiah 11:2-3 and Revelation 1:4-5, 3:1, 4:5, 5:6. What has the Spirit given the Lord?

Now read Revelation 2:7-8, 11, 17, 25-29 and 3:5-6, 10-13. What promises come to those who stand firm in the Lord?

How do we know this (Phil 1:6)?

Paul comments on the unity of the Spirit in a corporate setting. Standing firm as a body of believers carries the promises of the seven-fold Spirit's presence in the same way the Spirit led Jesus. Not only does Paul expect individual believers to walk according to the pattern, but he expects a *community of unity* where Christians help each other walk in the Spirit. Walking in the Spirit means the church will not have to endure the judgments or warnings the seven churches in Revelation heard. Believers keep their eyes on the Perfect Example, Jesus, fulfilling the law of love and enduring suffering.[2]

In Psalm 1, we see someone who has walked, stood, and sat with the wrong group. Believers become enemies of the cross when they grieve the Spirit, cause disunity, and follow a wrong pattern. Their witness is thwarted, their worship short-sighted, and their unity divided.

Read 1 Peter 5:9 and Jude 3. What is another word that demonstrates how we stand firm in unity with the Lord?

Unity can only happen when people remain firm in the faith. Standing firm implies *faithfulness*.

---

[1]   Guthrie, *New Testament Theology*, 636.

[2]   Ibid., 562, 568, 597, 661-63, 673.

Read Revelation 2:19, 13:10, 14:12; and, Philippians 4:1. What other things are tied to faithfulness?

A Dirge against Disunity and Envy: Singing Again in Minor Key (4:2-3)

In two favorite hymns, "Amazing Grace" and "It Is Well with My Soul," each has a verse with words that could easily modulate into a minor key. In "Amazing Grace" it is the third verse and in "It Is Well with My Soul" the first part of the second. Paul knows how to switch from major joyful sounds to minor mournful tunes and back again. As we have seen in chapter 3, he sang the dirge verse, the woes against false teachings. In the next few verses we see him return to a minor tone against disunity. The thing we need to see is that Paul uses the minor moods to emphasize the major keys. He wants a harmonious sound in the church and the minor keys prompt our attention.

Philippians 4:2-3. Paul takes the unity theme into the relationship between two women leaders in the church. The women had worked alongside Paul and struggled with him against persecution.

In these verses, Paul indicates the women have been struggling against each other. Rather than standing firm against the enemies of the cross and rather than walking in the Spirit as they had previously, they have become each other's enemy. Therefore, they are acting as enemies of the gospel, as enemies of the cross.

Already, Paul has urged both women and the whole church to agree in their minds (1:27; 2:3), feel about each other as he does for them (1:7; 2:1-4), and live in total harmony (2:2a; 3:16; 4:2).[3] Although the letter is not just to the two ladies, Paul wants these leaders to take the whole letter seriously in their own situation. Paul knows what their disharmony can do to his other "fellow workers" (4:3).

Based on Philippians 4:3, what promise can we believe even if we walk down a wrong path for awhile?

Paul has not stopped loving these women. They have been leaders: possibly opening their homes for church meetings, possibly helping establish the church, and possibly ministering as leaders in some other way. In 4:3, the Greek indicates they suffered alongside Paul by sharing the gospel.

Paul loves them just as he does everyone in the church: he calls them all his joy and his crown (4:1). He wants everyone to stand firm in the Lord, not in the path of erroneous teaching, strife, or earthly concerns. He calls on his "true companion"—the term could be a metaphor for the whole church or could be one person—to help Euodia and Syntyche restore the fellowship they once had.[4]

---

[3]   Hawthorne, *Philippians,* 177-78.

[4]   Ibid., 179-80.

Read Revelation 2:5, 16, 21-22; 3:3, 19; James 5:15-16; 1 John 1:9; and, Jude 20-21. How could the fellow worker(s) help the women?

What could the women do to restore their relationship?[5]

The literal meaning of asking his dear companion to help the women means that person or group is to take *hold of the women*. The brother was to help the ladies by bringing them together: taking a hand of one woman and a hand of the other one and pulling them close to each other. Imagine his taking those hands and putting them together.

Paul mentions Clement, another member who strove alongside him and the ladies. The importance of the Philippian Clement involves the corporate effects of Euodia's and Syntyche's argument. Paul uses these effects to point to the need of restoring the relationship.[6] Paul reminds the women of how they have worked with Clement and other believers. They have a common relationship with Christ. They have a common goal. They have to maintain that goal.

Reread Philippians 4:2-3 and 1:15-18. What attitude do you see in these verses?

We find the issue of envy here. That issue is very important in Philippians. Envy hinders joy and unity.

An Excursus on Envy

Some scholars believe envy gives a societal framework in the Bible which we in the West may not understand. These scholars think that envy only happens between people of equal status. Envy is tied to the honor/shame culture of the East or Middle East, somewhat like we see today. Rather than being an individualistic society which the West is, where honor and shame are more psychological and deal with personal worth, people in the East generally believe honor and shame affect social standing.[7]

Read 2 Samuel 12:1-7. Why would this story be so potent to David?

Read Mark 12:41-44 and Luke 21:1-4. Why would this be such a sacrifice for the widow?

---

[5]   Guthrie, *New Testament Theology*, 601.

[6]   Hawthorne, *Philippians,* 180-81; Silva, *Philippians*, 222-23.

[7]   Bruce J. Malina, *The New Testament World: Insights from Cultural Anthropology*, 3rd ed., rev. and exp. (Louisville: Westminster/John Knox Press, 2001).

Read Matthew 18:1-6, 19:13-15, and Mark 10:13-16. What would be significant about comparing Kingdom greatness, or Kingdom status, to children?

Envy arises with the amount of possessions people own. Acquiring more things would usually be hard. That fact makes the story of Nathan and David so potent. As king, David knew he was to protect the poor in his country. The poor owner did not have a way of gaining another lamb and the rich man selfishly had taken it.

In the NT, the widow had given all she had, with no promise of getting more. Still she was willing to give because of her love for God. Even though she did not know where she would get more money, she loved God enough to give what she had.

Comparing something as great as the Kingdom of God to children was asking the people to shift their views radically about greatness. Children in that day did not have status. Jesus was changing the mindset of the adults. He wanted people to understand that in order to be great in His kingdom, the listeners needed to accept servanthood as their new status. No one should envy another person's position.

Remember the illustration of Philippians 2:3 about the day laborer. The people were not to be in strife because of what another person was able to get at work. That also would apply to status in the church.

Within the community, stability and harmony in the family meant staying in one's societal boundaries. Envy would generally mean *distress at a peer's success*, so resentment could arise easily. The strength of the emotion might include the desire to take that person's possession, position, or reputation.[8] However because the church embraced people from every strata, envy could eventually cross societal lines.

James says that envy can occur towards anyone (Jas 2:1-14; 4:1-10). He indicates lust, envy, and bitter jealousy are problems in the church. He teaches that envy and strife should not be part of the fellowship (Jas 3:14).

In Philippians 2:6-11, when Paul teaches about Christ's emptying Himself of His glory, the apostle speaks against envy. Paul wants people to humble themselves as Christ did. In verse 6, Paul implies that the Lord did not envy His position, privileges, or possessions in heaven. Even though He knew He would not have a good status on earth, Christ chose to accept that position to raise the status of others. In Philippians 2:1-4, Paul has given the Philippians reasons to emulate the humility of Christ in their concern for other people.

Needless to say, envy does not portray love for God or people. Such was the case of Euodia and Syntyche. In their situation envy had ruled, not humility, joy, or love. Whatever may have been the cause, Paul did not take sides. He did not add to the feud by affirming one lady

---

[8] Malina, *The New Testament World*, 108-33; also, see Luke Timothy Johnson, *Brother of Jesus, Friend of God: Studies in the Letter of James* (Grand Rapids: William B. Eerdmans Publishing, 2004), 189-200, for more information on the subject of envy in the letter of James; contra Malina, see Timothy J. M. Ling, *The Judaean Poor and the Fourth Gospel* (Cambridge: Cambridge University Press, 2006). Reprinted with the permission of Cambridge University Press. Ling believes the church changed the social concept of envy and that the poor were more ready to help each other than Malina suggests.

more than the other. These ladies had been equal partners in the ministry of the gospel.[9] Paul encourages them to return to harmony and joy.

What causes you to envy or have jealousy?

Are you envious of people in the church?

Are you envious of their positions?

What do you need to do to keep unity in the community?

The Return to a Major Key (4:4-23)

Praising in Every Circumstance, Enjoying the Fruit of Peace

Philippians 4:4-7. To what theme does Paul return in 4:4-7 (See 3:1)?

Paul sandwiches 3:2-4:3 between 3:1 and 4:4-7 (an inclusio). He has had to demonstrate the ill effects of false teaching, inappropriate views of suffering, and internal disharmony. The worrisome characteristics in 3:2-4:3 would keep the people from taking care of others' welfare or rejoicing in the Lord.[10]

Instead of the worry and sour disharmony, believers are to consider the Lord's presence. Rather than worrying, feuding, or taking sides, the readers should remember that the Lord's return is near. Today we must consider that His return is an incentive to be gentle with each other. We should pray and praise with thanksgiving in every circumstance rather than let anything bring discord.

Read Isaiah 41:9-10. What encouragement for your peace does this give you?

Based on Philippians 4:4-7 and Isaiah 41:9-10, what excuse can we ever give for doing the *opposite* of what God asks of us in these verses?

With the Lord's Spirit always at hand, believers can rejoice in every circumstance (4:4), be gentle in visible ways (4:5), and pray about everything (4:6). Rather than focusing on the

---

[9]   Wenday Cotter, "Women's Authority Roles in Paul's Churches: Countercultural or Conventional?" *NovT* 36, no. 4 (October 1994: 353.

[10]   The word for *concern* in a positive sense in 2:20 is the same for *worry* in the negative in 4:6 (see Hawthorne, 183).

difficulties and negatives, the members can turn their focus onto God's peaceful presence. They can experience the Lord protecting their hearts and minds.[11] Remember that in 1:3-5, Paul has already given the entire church an example about praying with thanksgiving (4:6).

> Revisit Psalm 139:1-7, 23-24. Notice especially verses 2, 4, and 5. With Philippians 4:7 promising that God's peace guards our minds, what do the psalmist's words say to you?

> From what kinds of thoughts did the psalmist know God would guard his mind?

> In Philippians 4:7, we find that God's peace guards our hearts and minds in a specific location. Where?

Philippians 4:7 ties to 2:1-5 and reminds us of what we have in Christ and His Spirit. Our union with Christ gives us the place we can be sure of being heard, of receiving peace, and of having protection for our hearts and minds. Since the word for *mind* can also mean *thoughts*, we have permission to tell God what we think about our circumstances. The Lord knows those thoughts and those words before they are on our tongues, so we might as well tell Him.

We should tell God with an attitude of thanksgiving. We may not f-e-e-l thankful, but we can be obedient and give thanks. Just as the psalmist in 139 lists reasons to thank and praise the Lord and just as Paul lists good reasons for a gratitude attitude in Philippians 2:1-4, we can practice praise and thanks. Gratitude displays the characteristic of gentleness. When we pray and walk in the Spirit, we maintain an attitude of gratitude.

> Let's revisit Philippians 4:6. Notice four words for prayer. List them.

> How often do you obey the first two and the fourth, but do not practice the third?

> What does this verse say about prayer and anxiety?

> How does this verse help you work through the situations in your life?

When we pray with thanksgiving, even in tough circumstances, we place the trouble in God's hands. Thanking God for the answers ahead of time demonstrates an act of faith. We tell God we trust Him to handle our requests. Such action assists us in standing firm.

With this faith means we choose to believe what God says about our circumstances, rather than what the circumstances seem to say about God. By giving God the problem, thanking

---

[11]   Charles Bugg, "Philippians 4:4-7," *RevExp* 88, no. 3 (Summer 1991): 253-57.

Him in the situation, and believing Him for the answers, we let go of the worry. We open space in our lives for God's peace.

Let's look at another way Paul uses thanksgiving and praise. Read Ephesians 5:19-20 and Colossians 3:16. What does Paul say to do?

We have seen Paul sing in the tough times. We have gone over that fact a lot in this study. Paul sang songs, hymns, and spiritual songs to the Lord. We see in Ephesians 5:19-20 and Colossians 3:16 that he tells us to sing and *make melodies* in our hearts to the Lord.

The Psalms were the early church's hymnbook. Today our churches often use psalms in praise music. Paul may have sung some of the dirges in the hard times, but his heart seems to turn those laments into joyful sound almost all the time. Like Paul we are to find reasons to sing.

Earlier in this chapter, I mentioned the song "It Is Well with My Soul." You may know the story of how the song was written.

If you can, search the internet to find the story about Horatio G. Spafford. Write where he wrote the song:

After seeing the story, you may understand why he could have written a part of a verse that easily could be sung in a minor key. However, that was not Spafford's attitude. He was anything but sour. Although the first part of verse two could seem discordant, that section immediately flows into the next phrase which is one of rejoicing! Even after losing his business to a fire and his four daughters to shipwreck, he wrote a hymn about how blessed he was.

The verses of that song are very interesting. I did research on the hymn a few years ago when I was teaching a small group called "Songs, Hymns, and Spiritual Songs." I love all genres of music and enjoy the mixture of different genres in a worship service. I felt this hymn was important to use in that group.

When examining "It Is Well with My Soul" closely, I began to have Scripture verses pop into my head with each phrase of each stanza. I sensed that Spafford had a lot of Scripture memorized. Each phrase resembles a passage either from the OT or NT. I doubt he did a "Bible drill" when he composed the hymn. He did not have time to search for verses in his Bible to put into the song. Spafford wrote the song from a heart full of Scripture and his love for God.

Spafford was singing Scripture to the Lord in his grief!

We can imitate Paul and Spafford in our hard times. We can sing to the Lord the very words He inspired in His Word. We can make melodies that praise the Lord. That way certainly can provide protection for our hearts and minds, and can fill our souls with joy.

Let's connect 4:7 with 4:6. Notice the conjunction. Write it here:

The word *and* really means *and so*. This conjunction is not a conditional. It does not mean *only if* we thank God, He will guard our hearts and give us peace. God is not demanding we thank Him as the only requirement for answered prayer. However, "And so," or even better, "so" sets up the promise of peace *as* we pray.

The practice in verse 6 sets our hearts and minds in a right place to be guarded. When we thank God as we pray, we have the right climate for peace. Consider the following illustration.

Think of your favorite peaceful place. Describe it here:

My idea of peace is an idyllic picture I used to see every time we would drive to Estes Park, Colorado. There was a small lake not far from the side of the highway. Around the lake was beautiful meadowland. The water, grass, and flowers always seemed very calm. The place looked like a picture in a book.

However, the idea of peace in Philippians is that we have calm in the middle of a huge storm. We lived on the island of Guam for four years. Typhoons (hurricanes) would swirl around our home at least once a year. Our house was built like a bunker. We could sit in peace and not worry about the storm. While my home was in turbulent winds, I still could imagine I was in my idyllic place.

Read Philippians 4:4-7 aloud. Read it with feeling and put "so" at the beginning of verse 7.

Did you hear reasons to rejoice?   Can you say with Paul and Spafford, "It is well with my soul?"

In verse 7 the Greek term used for *the peace of God* is not used anywhere else in the NT. Paul uses a new phrase to impress his readers. Paul wants them to realize that the God of peace is the eternal God who sees the beginning from the end of the situation. He is the God available to those who pray (3:20-21; 4:5). This God, the Prince of Peace, through His Spirit of Peace infuses calm into our hearts with His very breath.

If you have ever seen gas filling a glass chamber (note: the gas has something in it to help us see it), describe here what that looks like.

In the gas experiment I once saw, the gas did not just rise in the glass or flow downward. The gas swirled and interwove within itself. It rolled around and created clouds which puffed until it filled the space.

With God's eternal self-peace—swirling and interweaving around as it fills us, covering the things that give us anxiety and filling the cracks caused by worry—we have little reason to focus on those issues of life. Such peace goes beyond anything we can comprehend. The peace is better than anything we can do to calm our own fears or relieve our own circumstances.

Right now, let's stop a minute.

Please hear me here: Let me take a moment to say I understand that sometimes we need to see a physician or a counselor to help with our peace. We may need medication or we may need to talk to someone who can assist us in reaching the state of calm. *At no time* am I saying that we are not to get help.

The Lord uses medicine. He also uses other people trained to encourage us to deal with issues that are too hard for us alone, or are too hard for our minds, bodies, and emotions to handle. This Bible study is to help us in our everyday situations *as much as possible*. Listen to the Lord about going for any medical or mental help you may need, and do not feel guilty when you get it.

Whatever the struggles, the battles and battlefield conditions, they can come under God's presence and peace. His presence is like a military guard.[12] God's peace protects our minds, offering emotional stability (4:1).

If we rejoice in the Lord, show the fruit of gentleness, stop worrying, and express thankfulness, we have less room for discouragement, dissention, or disharmony.[13] Hmmm . . . now that is a heart-ful and a head-ful, onto which we *can* grasp and cling!

Reread 3:20-21. What in these verses helps us with the proper mindset and gives victory over worry?

Paul introduces that hymn piece to promote unity. With this glorious chorus, believers can rest assured that as they await the Savior, they have hope. Therefore today we have the confidence that through Christ's power He will subject *all things* under His control now and in the future, and give us His peace as we wait.

Reread 4:6 five times. Only each time, substitute one of the following words for "praise":

first, use praise
then, honor
then, glorification
then, exultation
then, magnification.

---

[12] Hawthorne, *Philippians*, 184-85.
[13] Ibid., 184.

How does rereading with a different word affect your peace, hope, and confidence?

How does it help you pray with thanksgiving?

The Greek word for *thanksgiving* or praise in 4:6 is *eucharistia*. We get the word *Eucharist* from it. In the Eucharist, we give deep devotion to the Lord for all He has done for us. In the same way we praise the Lord during His Supper (Communion), we are to *express our gratitude*—all the time.

While we may not feel thankful for our circumstances, we can praise Him anyway as the One who has given us life and who will work through our situation. We can thank Him as a way to express faith in His peace. We can recognize His presence and appreciate His love and concern. We present our petitions to the Lord who has promised His daily presence, His peace, His transformation, and His control. Those facts infuse our prayer life with PRAISE!

Praise the Lord for what He has done in your life:

1. for taking you on the right path;
2. for taking you through suffering;
3. for everything you have for life and godliness.

Philippians 4:8-9. List the ways God guards our hearts and minds.

One author says that anxiety has a good purpose: it causes us to "make hope wise ... not just 'to learn how to hope ... but to learn how to hope in danger.'"[14] With the peaceful presence of God and the prospect of Christ's coming again for us, we have hope no matter what happens. The One who keeps our hearts and minds will take care of the issues that hurt and harass us.[15]

People reject us and hurt us; life hands us medical diagnoses we do not want to hear; we lose our jobs. God reminds us to view those situations through the lens of His resurrection power. We can look at each thing according to the virtues that Paul lists in Philippians 4:8, and the fact that the God of peace is with us (4:9).

Christ has overcome the hurts and given us hope. I like the definition of hope from Indonesia. The Indonesians define hope: "to look beyond the horizon."[16]

Take a situation that you are experiencing in your life right now. Write it here.

---

[14] Jürgen Moltmann, *The Coming of God: Christian Eschatology*, trans. Margaret Kohl (Minneapolis: Fortress Press, 2004), 234.

[15] Beth Moore, *So Long Insecurity: You've Been a Bad Friend to Us* (Carol Stream, IL: Tyndale House Publishers, 2010), 80; Moltmann, *The Coming of God*, 233-34.

[16] Moltmann, *The Coming of God*, 234.

Have you been anxious about it?

How have you *looked beyond the horizon* to make a specific petition to God—with gratitude?

I mentioned previously that we can come boldly before the throne of grace at any time (Heb 4:16), but I do believe God prefers the gratitude attitude when we come. We, as believers in Christ, can bring our troubles, our worries, our heartaches, even our envy, to the Lord. We can say with Martin Luther that "even if he knew that the world was going to end tomorrow,"[17] he would plant an apple tree today. Such a feat demonstrates looking beyond the horizon and taking action to assess the circumstances the way Paul has done.[18]

Look more closely at the list of virtues that Paul puts in 4:8:[19]

True—whatever things—especially of things spoken—are dependable.

Honorable—whatever things, or characteristics, are holy or above reproach.

Right—whatever things are conforming to requirements of justice, are equitable.

Pure—whatever is pure, as pure as everything belonging to God.

Lovely—whatever causes delight, is pleasing or agreeable.

Worthy of Praise—whatever is commendable.

Excellent—whatever is of excellent character or distinguished merit, worthy of commendation or praise (See the commentary on Philippians 1:10.).

Read Philippians 4:8-9. What does Paul say to do with these things?

Paul says to dwell on—to think carefully or deeply on these virtues—and practice them. *Thinking carefully* means *to ponder them*, *to meditate* on them. We love the Lord with our minds when we let our minds dwell on the virtues of 4:8. These items should fill our minds so little room exists for the wrong kinds of thoughts.

Go back to the situation you mentioned on the last page. Answer each question below according to the virtues of 4:8—meditate on your circumstance with each virtue:

---

17   Ibid., 235.

18   Ibid.

19   *BDAG*, s. v. ἀληθής, σεμνός, δίκαιος, ἁγνός, προσφιλής, εὔφημος, ἀσρετή, and ἔπαινος.

What is true about or within the situation?

What is honorable?

What is right?

What is pure?

What is lovely?

What is worthy of praise?

Is there any excellence?

Is there anything worthy of commendation?

As you have dwelled or meditated on the positives in your situation, what have you found that helped you have a better attitude of gratitude?

Why?

What qualities could you *not find* in your situation?

If you view the situation from God's perspective and if you look at the circumstance with the view of God's guarding your heart, how would those two ideas help you see positives and give you gratitude?

Read 1 Thessalonians 5:16-18. What does this say about your situation?

Reread Philippians 4:9. What things have you *learned* from Paul in this Philippian study?

What things have you *received* from him?

What things have you *heard and seen* in him?

Which of these things have you put into practice?

How did you sense the God of peace was with you?

Now return to Philippians 1:10. How do you think Paul's prayer for you has been answered through the study of Philippians?

Trusting the Lord for Provisions

Philippians 4:10-14. The inclusio of verses 10 and 14 is Paul's way of thanking the Philippians for their help. They had desired to help earlier. They had not been able to do so for a long time.

In 4:10 and 14, what did Paul say about the Philippians' not being able to give previously?

Inserted between 10 and 14 are pearls of wisdom about that time. Beside each reference, state how Paul's *attitude of gratitude* helped him:

4:11:

4:12:

4:13:

The image of Paul as a day laborer is not new to us. We know Paul purposely did not take money from many people. Even though some Corinthians berated him as an apostle because he did not accept their patronage, Paul chose not to live in abundance on his missionary journeys. He certainly did not live lavishly in prison. He may have lived more luxuriously at some point in his life, because he says in 4:12 that he knows how to live in prosperity. However, riches no longer are of upmost importance to him.[20]

What does Paul say about living in prosperity?

Evaluate his view of poverty?

In verses 4:11-13 what is the key to Paul's outlook?

In 4:14 what does Paul call his situation?

Regardless of the "affliction"—*trial* or *hardship*, we know Paul has learned to rejoice (4:10). We know he is thankful in his situation whatever that may be. We know Paul could appreciate whatever God would do for him. He could sing and make a melody in his heart at any time.

As I was driving home from the seminary library one afternoon, I listened to Jill Briscoe's program on KCBI, a station in the Fort Worth-Dallas area. Jill was speaking from Philippians 4. She called Philippians, "a 'dancing letter.'"[21]

At the end of the message, she mentioned an experience she had when she was visiting a missionary in Africa several years earlier. She, the missionary, and some of the women from the church were walking through the jungle. After a little while, they heard singing coming from the other direction.

The missionary said that those were Christians coming towards them. Jill asked how the missionary knew that. The lady answered that the church in Africa is a singing church. Then the missionary told about a man who had come to her husband. He did not ask to be saved; he did not ask to join the church. He told the missionary pastor, "I want to sing." Paul would understand that. He would want us to understand that.

Paul says he had learned how to be content. I wonder if, when trials started, Paul usually began to sing—we know he did in Philippi—*in jail*, and in Rome—*in jail*.

Read the following passages. Beside each one, tell a) what the people did, b) how God/Jesus responded, and c) what ultimately happened:

Numbers 12:1-16:

a.

b.

---

[20] Paul Barnett, *Jesus and the Rise of Early Christianity: A History of New Testament Times* (Downers Grove, IL: IVP Academic, 1999), 260-61.

[21] Jill Briscoe, "Telling the Truth," *KCBI*, (6 May 2010), also under http://www.kcbi.org/index.cfm?fuseaction=programguide (accessed 6 May 2010). Used by permission from Telling the Truth, the Bible teaching ministry of the Briscoes, (October 2011).

c.

Numbers 14:20-35:

a.
b.
c.

Numbers 16:1-35:

a.
b.
c.

Numbers 20:1-13:

a.
b.
c.

Numbers 21:4-9:

a.
b.
c.

Deuteronomy 6:13-16:

a.
b.
c.

Luke 4:9-13:

a.
b.
c.

John 6:41-51:

a.
b.
c.

1 Corinthians 10:6-13:

a.

b.

c.

Ephesians 4:29-32:

a.

b.

c.

What happened to the Israelites and Moses when they tested God, griped against Him, or complained against His appointed leaders?

What does Jesus say about our testing the Lord?

How does Paul interpret the story and the punishment in 1 Corinthians 10?

In what context do we see Paul teaching us not to grieve the Holy Spirit?

In Ephesians 4:30, the word for *grieve* means to *irritate, offend,* or *insult*. This interpretation implies *testing* God's Spirit. This command seems to echo the picture of Numbers and 1 Corinthians.

When we usually consider the concept about grieving the Holy Spirit, we may think of making Him *sad*. Instead we make the Spirit *mad*. When we gripe against the Lord and do not speak in love for others, we do not trust Him to work in our circumstances or through other people.

Okay, yes, the psalmists and prophets told God how they felt and we can as well. However, the kind of griping Paul discourages is the *sin of disbelief* against God and *arrogance* against our neighbor. We do not dwell on the goodness of God, trust His indwelling Spirit to care for us, or treat our neighbors with respect when we gripe.

Contentment or complaint—we have a choice: sing or gripe. Griping does not open prison doors (Acts 16). Contentment and singing seem to have the better effect. At least, those two features have an effect on the singer. Both the attitude and the action open the doors of our hearts to a gratitude attitude, rather than keeping our minds in the dungeon of despair.

I wish I were consistent with singing and not griping. At one point in Benny's ministry, someone said something to him in front of our children (See the pattern in my life about my kids?). It was horribly mean. I will not share the details of what was said, but I will illustrate how I handled the situation. *I did not sing.*

I felt like slamming doors and shouting in anger. My reaction was anything but what the Lord wanted my children to see. I was telling God how I felt, but I was not content in my situation. The audacity of that person speaking to my husband in that way was bad enough, but saying it in front of our children added more insult to the injury. That person did not love my husband or my children as the Lord commands, but neither did I love that person. I was livid.

I wish I had sung. While my children needed to see I loved them enough to want to protect them, my attitude did not honor the Lord. I wish it had. I regret that I did not model the kind of forgiveness my kids needed to see. I wish I had been more like I was in my next example.

One time as I flew home from North Carolina, I had all kinds of flight problems: weather, delayed flights, uncertainty of making the connecting flight to Dallas-Fort Worth, not wanting to get an expensive hotel room, etc. The whole trip kept me awake over twenty-four hours. While at the first airport, I emailed a prayer request asking people to pray about the storms and flights. I actually did not panic and I did not get angry about the situation. I had opportunities to minister to four women during the hours of waiting in both airports and on the planes.

One even said, "You are so calm about this." Even if she did not know the Lord personally, she had learned about my PhD studies in New Testament. I needed to portray a good testimony!

That morning a woman, in the Sunday Bible class which our son-in-law had taught, prayed that the Lord would use me in the airport. Her prayer remained on my mind, and I hoped my attitude about the planes did not detract from my witness. I had the help of prayers from that woman, my family, my Bible study group, and my friends—prayers which encouraged me during the mess.

I could have worried. Like my earlier experience when I did not sing, I could have complained and not appreciated the help of all the prayers for peace. I could have chosen to gripe. While I wish I could say I have the right mindset all the time, I know the Lord answered prayers for a proper focus that day and night because of the help of others.

The flight was to have a layover in Atlanta. While on the plane, I said, "Lord, I am writing and teaching about contentment in *all things*, about rejoicing and giving thanks in *all things*. I can see this situation as affliction and bemoan my circumstance. I can gripe and grieve You, *or* I can give this to You with thanksgiving." How precious when we choose contentment rather than complaint. How thankful I was for the help through prayer.

Return to Philippians 4:10-14. How does Paul receive the Philippians' help?

We included 2 Corinthians 8:1-6 earlier when we discussed Philippians 1:7. Let's remind ourselves what Paul says about the Macedonians in these verses:

In 2 Corinthians 8:4, what is the Macedonians' attitude towards giving?

How eager are the Macedonians to give?

Read 1 Corinthians 3:1-3, 9:15-18; 2 Corinthians 2:14-17, 8:1-12, 9:1- 4, 10:7-9, 11:7-31; and Philippians 4:18. What else does Paul call the Macedonians' gift?

We can see why Paul would accept the Macedonians' help and not the Corinthians'. Their outlooks toward giving reflect *what* they would receive. Their attitudes toward giving also reflect their attitudes *about* receiving.

Complete the chart:

Attitude of Receiving

Macedonians'   **Corinthians'**

As Paul considered the Macedonians' gift (4:10-18), he probably had the Corinthian letters in mind and the serious confrontations with that church over gifts and apostleship. When he thanked the Philippians, he showed his true appreciation for their mindset towards giving. The Philippians' humility and living sacrifice prompted Paul to accept their strong plea to help him. The people reflected the sweet aroma in their commitment to the Lord and to the koinonia of the gospel. This aroma was what Paul had wanted the Corinthians to display in giving and receiving.

Philippians 4:15-18. In 2 Corinthians 11:8-9, how many times do the Macedonians help Paul?

What have you learned about receiving from Philippians 4:15-18 and 2 Corinthians 11:8-9?

Have you ever considered that if you do not receive, you may be *subtracting* or *stealing* from someone's spiritual account?

How do you feel about the last question?

Philippians 4:17 uses banking or commercial language. Their gift is a credit, a plus in the column of their spiritual account. Literally, Paul says, "I desire fruit that increases what is said about you." By giving, the Philippians have continued the partnership of advancing the gospel (1:5), of increasing of their love (1:9), and of growing in their faith (1:25).

Giving for the right reasons always enhances the life of the giver. Because givers are in partnership with receivers, believers also must help others grow by receiving their gifts. We believers should not want to remove, subtract, or steal an opportunity from someone.

Possibly we feel guilty when people give us things or do something for us. We may feel we don't deserve the gift or that we have more than the person giving. Paul says he has more than enough (4:18).

By receiving, Paul has accepted the gift as a "spiritual investment."[22] The gift would continue to pay compound interest with rich dividends for the giver. Paul considers that helping people grow is a part of *his* "eschatological 'reward'"[23] and "their gift to him has the effect of accumulating 'interest' toward their eschatological reward."[24] Paul spends time encouraging the ones who would receive a plus in their reward column for helping him. He would not want to "steal" from their account.

Givers and receivers carry both the privilege and responsibility of their choices and attitudes. Not receiving can steal from the mutual investment that reaches others for Christ; can steal from the account or "interest" of those giving; can steal from the fruit, or testimony, of what is said about their giving; can steal the results by discouraging the givers—especially those who still need to mature in Christ; and can steal by disparaging the partnership.[25] As we give graciously, we also can receive graciously.

Philippians 4:19. After he commends the Philippians for giving, what does Paul say concerning his need?

Reread 2 Corinthians 8:1, 9. What would be the reason Paul could say what he does in Philippians 4:19?

What do these Philippians and Corinthians verses have in common?

---

[22] Hawthorne, *Philippians*, 205-6.

[23] Gordon D. Fee, *Philippians*, The IVPNTC, eds. Grant R. Osborne, D. Stuart Briscoe, and Haddon Robinson (Downers Grove, IL: InterVarsity Press, 1999), 190.

[24] Ibid.

[25] Hendriksen, *Exposition of Philippians*, 207-8; F. F. Bruce, *Philippians*, 154; Hawthorne, *Philippians*, 205-6; Fee, *Philippians*, 190.

Another Doxology

Philippians 4:20. Paul does it again. He rejoices. He breaks into song. What does he sing this time?

What do we see in 4:10-19 that could tell us why he breaks into song?

How could the Philippians be sure they would have their own needs supplied?

This doxology reminds us of other doxologies in Paul's letters. Paul cannot praise the Lord enough for His provisions. God the Father would supply all of Paul's and the Philippians' needs from His storehouse, the one which holds the riches of His glory.

Read the following verses. Write the specific reasons or ways Paul praises the Lord:

Romans 11:36:

Galatians 1:5:

Ephesians 3:20-21:

1 Timothy 1:17:

These are not all the doxologies that Paul has written, but what is the common theme in these selections?

What has reading these verses done for you?

Spend time praising the Lord by praying each of these four verses to Him. What did praising the Lord in this way do for you?

Your sweet-smelling aroma and sacrifice involves trusting God for His provisions. Just as Paul and the Philippians could know that God would supply all their needs, we can as well. How awesome is our God the Provider!

Singing a Song of Farewell

Philippians 4:21-22. Compare 4:21-22 with 1:1-2. Write what you see.

Paul ends the letter of Philippians the same way he began it, consequently forming an inclusio of greetings. Paul ties his love for the people to his desire that they greet each other in the same way he has greeted them. Some believers may not have been speaking to each other at all. Paul stresses his positive mandate: "Greet *every* saint." Greeting someone meant blessing that person. The members were not to let envy and disharmony continue, but they were to model unity by blessing each other joyfully.

What is the significance of Paul's emphasis on greetings in his farewell?

How many times does Paul use the word "greet"?

Whom does Paul include as people sending greetings to the Philippians?

Paul incorporates the greetings of all the believers around him. A significant emphasis in these verses includes *the saints in Caesar's household*. The word *household* includes more people than just Caesar's family members or slaves. Personal servants, free men, officials managing the home and government, and soldiers assigned to the palace could be a part of the group.[26]

We do not have a definitive description of all the people in Caesar's palace who became Christians, but those believers would understand the struggle to stand firm in unity and live with joy in spite of persecution. Their reassurance and support could help the Philippians stand firm in trials since Paul and the believers in Caesar's palace could. The Philippians' participation with Paul essentially advanced the gospel in Caesar's house, and now members of that household want to encourage them.[27]

Another part of the inclusio is *grace*. Paul ends as he began, with a word of encouragement. That encouragement comes through the grace of God the Father and of the Lord Jesus. Grace includes the joy the Father and Son give.

One more question before we close (Remember what Jill Briscoe called this letter.). How has Philippians given you reason "to sing" or "to dance"?

---

[26]   Fee, *Philippians*, 196; Hawthorne, *Philippians*, 281; O'Brien, *The Epistle to the Philippians, 554;*
Melick, Philippians, Colossians, Philemon, 159.

[27]   Ibid.

Conclusion: A Reminder to Sing

Paul writes to commend the Philippians for their participation in spreading the Gospel. Although he is more positive with this letter than in Corinthians and Galatians, Paul does have concerns for the church in Philippi. He reminds his readers that they need to remain faithful to his teachings about Jesus. The Philippians must stand firm in difficult circumstances. They need to be careful not to accept wrong theology. Their witness must remain free of envy and friction. They must model humility and unity. They need to sing with joy.

Paul opens and closes the letter with joyful greetings, reminders of his love for the people, positive exhortations for faithfulness, and songs of praise and thanksgiving. The letter is full of joy and rejoicing. Paul provides the example of what to do in trials, the right attitude when things go wrong, and the pattern of how to live in unity. His song-filled life offers assurance that people can sing in every way every day about every situation.

The message Paul has given the Philippians he gives us today. He delights when people live together in harmony. He encourages love for God and people. Paul wants a joyful witness and unified community. In the same way he asked his readers in the first century, he would ask us to fill his cup of joy and join in his lifesong.

My Song of Thanksgiving: An Epilogue

As we close the study, let me say with Paul: "The grace of the Lord Jesus be with your spirit." Thank you for sharing this study with me. I pray the Lord adds to your accounts with compound interest because you have graciously received this study and partnered with me: We have shared in the gospel.

I pray you are able to dance even more. I pray you are able to sing even louder. I pray you are able to rejoice more often. Let's praise the Lord as Paul does: "Now to our God and Father be glory forever and ever. Amen" (4:20).

About the Author

Sharon Gresham speaks, writes, and sings. Her ministry exists from her experiences as a wife, mother, pastor's wife, school teacher, and missionary. Sharon's background of brokenness leads her to speak from her heart on forgiveness and freedom in Christ. She infuses Bible study, humor, love for people, and her own circumstances in sharing how others also can be free.

Sharon is a prayer warrior who believes in the power of prayer. She listens to others and delights in praying for them. She enjoys working with people, listening to their needs, and encouraging them in a personal relationship with the Lord Jesus Christ.

A graduate of Christian Leaders and Speakers' Services (CLASS) and formerly with MORE HOURS IN MY DAY, Sharon is a gifted and genuine speaker. Her skills of 38 years show the maturity of time and experience. Her love of the Lord leads others into growth opportunities. Her easy style encourages her listeners, while her dramatic approach engages them.

Sharon writes Bible studies, devotional materials, articles, poetry, music, and academic material. She is a published author. She has written and led ladies' retreats, and spoken to youth and children in chapels and camps. Sharon has worked with youth many years. She has led Bible studies with youth, singles, and married adults. She has spoken to prison groups. She has sung with Southwestern Baptist Theological Seminary (SWBTS) Oratorio Chorus, Fort Worth, TX, and The Singing Churchwomen of Oklahoma.

Sharon graduated from Southwestern Baptist Theological Seminary with a Masters of Arts in Theology in 2008. She earned the equivalent of a double major in Biblical Studies and Systematic Theology. She currently pursues a PhD in Scripture and Witness from B. H. Carroll Theological Institute, Arlington, TX. Her studies in the field of New Testament include her major in Biblical Theology.

Sharon is the wife of Benny, mother of two married adults, and grandmother of six. She and Benny have ministered in the United States, Guam, and South Korea. Both possess a heart for the world, and mobilize Christians to be on mission with God.

Bibliography

Alexander, W. L. *Deuteronomy*. The Pulpit Commentary, eds. H. D. M. Spence and Joseph S. Excell. New York: Funk and Wagnalls, 1950.

Barnett, Paul. *Jesus and the Rise of Early Christianity: A History of New Testament Times*. Downers Grove, IL: IVP Academic, 1999.

Barth, Karl. *The Epistle to the Philippians*. Richmond: John Knox Press, 1947.

Bauer, Walter, Frederick William Danker, Kurt and Barbara Aland, and F. W. Gingrich, eds. *A Greek-English Lexicon of the New Testament and Early Christian Literature*. 3rd ed. Chicago: The University of Chicago Press, 2000.

Briscoe, Jill. "Telling the Truth." *KCBI* (6 May 2010). http://www.kcbi.org/index.cfm?fuseaction=programguide (accessed 6 May 2010).

Broomall, Wick. "Type, Typology." In *Baker's Dictionary of Theology*, ed. Everett F. Harrison, 533-34. Grand Rapids: Baker Book House, 1979.

Bruce, F. F. *The Epistle to the Hebrews*. Grand Rapids: Wm. B. Eerdmans Publishing, 1979.

———. *Philippians*. NIBC, ed. W. Ward Gasque. Peabody, MA: Hendrickson Publishers, 1989.

Bugg, Charles. "Philippians 4:4-7." *RevExp* 88, no. 3 (Summer 1991): 253-57.

Bullinger, E. W. *Figures of Speech Used in the Bible*. Grand Rapids: Baker Book House, 1968.

Cohen, Jeffrey M. "Love of Neighbor and its Antecedent Verses." *JBQ* 24, no. 1 (January-March 1996): 19.

Cotter, Wenday. "Women's Authority Roles in Paul's Churches: Countercultural or Conventional?" *NovT* 36, no. 4 (October 1994): 350-72.

Davidson, A. B. *The Theology of the Old Testament*, ed. S. D. F. Salmond. ITL. New York: Charles Scribner's Sons, 1907.

Derrett, J. Duncan M. "Short Comments: 'Love thy neighbor as a man like thyself'?" *ExpT* 83, no. 2 (November 1971): 55-6.

Dodd, Brian J. *The Problem with Paul*. Downers Grove: InterVarsity Press, 1996.

Fee, Gordon D. *God's Empowering Presence: The Holy Spirit in the Letter of Paul*. Peabody, MA: Hendrickson Publishers, 2002.

_____ . *Pauline Christology: An Exegetical-Theological Study*. Peabody, MA: Hendrickson Publishers, 2007.

_____ . *Paul's Letter to the Philippians*. Grand Rapids: William B. Eerdmans Publishing Company, 1995.

_____ . *Philippians*. The IVPNTC, eds. Grant R. Osborne, D. Stuart Briscoe, and Haddon Robinson. Downers Grove, IL: InterVarsity Press, 1999.

Gorman, Michael J. *Apostle of the Crucified Lord: A Theological Introduction to Paul and His Letters*. Grand Rapids: William B. Eerdmans, 2004.

Green, Joel B. *The Gospel of Luke*. NICNT, ed. Ned B. Stonehouse, F. F. Bruce, and Gordon D. Fee. Grand Rapids: William B. Eerdmans, 1997.

Gresham, Sharon L. "Fulfilling the Law through Love: Romans 13:8-10." *Romans*, prof. Dr. John Taylor. Fort Worth: Southwestern Baptist Theological Seminary, an unpublished paper (April 1, 2008).

_____ . "Philippians." *Hermeneutics*, prof. Dr. William B. Tolar. Fort Worth: Southwestern Baptist Theological Seminary: an unpublished paper (2003).

_____ . "Unpublished Class Notes." *Letters to 1-2 Timothy and Titus*, prof. Dr. Paul Wolf. Fort Worth: Southwestern Baptist Theological Seminary (May 18, 2007).

Guthrie, Donald. *New Testament Theology*. Downers Grove, IL: Inter-Varsity Press, 1981.

Hagner, Donald A. *Matthew 14-28*. WBC 33B, eds. David A. Hubard, Glenn W. Barker, and Raph P. Martin. Dallas: Word Books, Publisher, 1995.

Hartley, John E. *Leviticus*. WBC 4, ed. David A. Hubbard and John D. W. Watts. Dallas: Word Books, 1992.

Hawthorne, Gerald F. *Philippians*. WBC 43, ed. Bruce M. Metzger, Ralph P. Martin, and Lynn Allan Losie. Waco: Word Books, 1983.

Hendriksen, William. *Exposition of Philippians*. New Testament Commentary 6. Grand Rapids: Baker Book House, 1962.

Hewitt, Hugh. *The Embarrassed Believer: Reviving Christian Witness in an Age of Unbelief*. Nashville: Word Publishing, 1998.

Hoehner, Harold W. "Ephesians." In *Bible Knowledge Commentary: New Testament*, ed. John F. Walvoord, and Roy B. Zuck, 632. Wheaton: Scripture Press, 1983; now under David C. Cook. Publisher permission required to reproduce.

Hunter, Archibald M. *The Letter of Paul to the Philippians*. LBC, ed. Balmer H. Kelly. Richmond: John Knox Press, 1959.

Johnson, Luke Timothy. *Brother of Jesus, Friend of God: Studies in the Letter of James*. Grand Rapids: William B. Eerdmans Publishing, 2004.

Landriot, Monsignor. *Conferences on the Holy Spirit*, trans. T.T. Carter. Oxford: A. R. Mowbray and Company, 1899.

Lane, William L. *The Gospel according to Mark*. NICNT, ed. Ned B. Stonehouse, F. F. Bruce, and Gordon D. Fee. Grand Rapids: William B. Eerdmans Publishing, 1974.

Lea, Thomas D., and Hayne P. Griffin, Jr. *1, 2 Timothy, and Titus*. NAC 34, ed. David S. Dockery, et al. Nashville: Broadman Press, 1992.

Lenski, R. C. H. *The Interpretation of St. Paul's Epistles to the Galatians, to the Ephesians, and to the Philippians*. Minneapolis: Augsburg Publishing House, 1961.

Ling, Timothy J. M. *The Judaean Poor and the Fourth Gospel*. Cambridge: Cambridge University Press, 2006.

Luther, Martin. *Lectures on Romans: Glosses and Scolia*, ed. Hilton C. Oswald, trans. Walter G. Tillmanns (Chaps 1-2), trans. Jacob A. O. Preus (Chaps 3-16). *LW* 25. Saint Louis: Concordia Publishing House, 1972.

MacArthur, John, Jr. *Hebrews*. The MacArthur New Testament Commentary. Chicago: Moody Press, 1983.

Malamat, Abraham. "'Love Your Neighbor as Yourself': What It Really Means." *BAR* 16, no. 4 (July-August 1990): 50.

Malina, Bruce J. *The New Testament World: Insights from Cultural Anthropology*. 3rd ed. Rev. and exp. Louisville: Westminster/John Knox Press, 2001. www.wjkbooks.com.

Mann, C. S. *Mark*. AB 27, eds. William F. Albright and David N. Freedman. Garden City: Doubleday & Company, Inc., 1986.

Martin, Ralph P. *The Epistle of Paul to the Philippians*. Grand Rapids: William B. Eerdmans Publishing 1988.

———. *Worship in the Early Church*. Grand Rapids: William B. Eerdmans Publishing Company, 1998.

Maxwell, John C. *Deuteronomy*. The Preacher's Commentary Series 5, ed. Lloyd J. Ogilvie. Nashville: Thomas Nelson Publishers, 1987.

McBeth, J. P. *Exegetical and Practical Commentary on the Epistle to the Romans*. New York: Fleming H. Revell Company, 1937.

McDonald, Larry S. *The Merging of Theology and Spirituality: An Examination of the Life and Work of Alister E. McGrath*. Lanham, MD: University Press of America, Inc., 2006.

Melick, Richard R., Jr. *Philippians, Colossians, Philemon*. NAC 32. Nashville: Broadman Press, 1991.

Merrill, Eugene H. *Deuteronomy*. NAC 4, eds. E. Ray Clendenen and Kenneth A. Matthews. Nashville: Broadman & Holman, 1994.

Miller, Calvin. *Into the Depths of God: Where Eyes See the Invisible, Ears Hear the Inaudible, and Minds Conceive the Inconceivable*. Minneapolis: Bethany House Publishers, 2000.

Moberly, R. W. L. "Toward an Interpretation of the Shema." In *Theological Exegesis: Essays in Honor of Brevard S. Childs*, eds. Christopher Seitz and Kathryn Greene-McCreight, 124-144. Grand Rapids: William B. Eerdmans Publishing, 1999.

Moo, Douglas J. *The Letter of James*. PNTC, ed. D. A. Carson. Grand Rapids: William B. Eerdmans Publishing, 2000.

Moore, Beth. *Get Out of That Pit: Straight Talk about God's Deliverance from a Former Pit Dweller*. Nashville: Integrity Publishers, 2007.

————. *So Long Insecurity: You've Been a Bad Friend to Us*. Carol Stream, IL: Tyndale House Publishers, 2010.

Moses, Jan. "God Will Make a Way." Fort Worth: an unpublished email, N. D.

Moses, Mark. *An Uncommon Faith: The Story of Missionary Jan Moses and Her Journey with Cancer*. Garland, TX: Hannibal Books, 2007.

Moule, H. C. G. *Studies in Philippians*. Grand Rapids: Kregel Publications, 1977.

Mulholland, M. Robert, Jr. "Social Criticism." In *Interpreting the New Testament: Essays on Methods and Issues*, ed. David Alan Black and David S. Dockery, 170-86. Nashville: Broadman & Holman Publishers, 2001.

Müller, Jac. J. *The Epistles of Paul to the Philippians and to Philemon*. NICNT, ed. Ned B. Stonehouse, F. F. Bruce, and Gordon D. Fee. Grand Rapids: Wm. B. Eerdmans Publishing Company 1955.

Moltmann, Jürgen. *The Coming of God: Christian Eschatology*, trans. Margaret Kohl. Minneapolis: Fortress Press, 2004.

New Greek-English Interlinear New Testament, trans. Robert K. Brown and Philip Wesley Comfort, ed. J. D. Douglas. Carol Stream, IL: Tyndale House Publishers, 1990.

Neudecker, Reinhard. "'And You Shall Love Your Neighbor as Yourself—I Am the Lord' (Lev 19,18) in Jewish Literature." *Biblica* 73, no. 4 (1992): 505.

Newman, Barclay M., Jr. *A Concise Greek-English Dictionary of the New Testament.* Stuttgart: Deutsche Bibelgesellschaft, 1993.

Neyrey, Jerome H. "Lost in Translation: Did It Matter if Christians 'Thanked' God or Gave 'God Glory'?" *CBQ* 71, no. 1 (January 2009): 1-23. FirstSearch. http://firstsearch.oclc.org/ (accessed 4 January 2009).

O'Brien, Peter T. *The Epistle to the Philippians: A Commentary on the Greek Text.* NIGTC, eds. I. Howard Marshall and W. Ward Gasque. Grand Rapids: William B. Eerdmans Publishing, 1991.

Pearson, Calvin. "Philippians 1." A Taped Sermon at Chapel. Fort Worth: Southwestern Baptist Theological Seminary (01 November 2008). http://www.swbts.edu/events/chapel_archive.cfm (accessed 01 November 2008).

Peterlin, Davorin. *Paul's Letter to the Philippians in the Light of Disunity in the Church.* NovTSup 79, ed. A. J. Malherbe and D. P. Moessner. Leiden: E. J. Brill, 1995.

Piper, John. "A Mind in Love with God: The Private Life of a Modern Evangelical." An *Outside Events* conference (3 July 1997). *desiringGod,* http://www.desiringgod.org/ (accessed 13 October 2011). Used by Permission from *desiringGod.*

Rivadeneira, Caryn. "Leading Your Enemies." *Gifted for Leadership. Christianity Today.* http://todayschristianwomanstore.com/leyoen.html (accessed 27 February 2010).

Robertson, A. T. *Paul's Joy in Christ: Studies in Philippians.* New York: Fleming H. Revell Company, 1917.

————. *Word Pictures in the New Testament. WordSearch* Program.

Rogers, Cleon L., Jr., and Rogers, Cleon L., III. *The New Linguistic and Exegetical Key to the Greek New Testament.* Grand Rapids: ZondervanPublishingHouse, 1998.

Schreiner, Thomas R. *Paul: Apostle of God's Glory in Christ: A Pauline Theology.* Downers Grove, IL: InterVarsity Press, 2001.

Scott, J. Julius, Jr., *Jewish Backgrounds of the New Testament.* Grand Rapids: Baker Books, 1995.

Silva, Moisés. *Philippians.* BECNT, ed. Moisés Silva. Grand Rapids: Baker Book House, 1992.

Stanglin, Keith D. "The Historical Connection between the Golden Rule and the Second Greatest Command." *JRE* 33, no. 2 (June 2005): 360-1.

Sumney, Jerry L. *Philippians: A Greek Student's Intermediate Reader*. Peabody, MA: Hendrickson Publishers, 2007.

Thuren, Lauri "Was Paul Angry?: Derhetorizing Galatians." In *The Rhetorical Interpretation of Scripture: Essays from the 1996 Malibu Conference*, eds. Stanley E. Porter and Dennis L. Stamps, 302-30. JSNTSup 180, ed. Stanley E. Porter. Sheffield: Sheffield Academic Press, 1999.

Towner, Philip H. *The Letters to Timothy and Titus*. NICNT, eds. Ned NB. Stonehouse, F. F. Bruce, and Gordon D. Fee. Grand Rapids: William B. Eerdmans Publishing, 2006.

Tozer, A. W. *The Pursuit of God: The Human Thirst for the Divine*. Camp Hill, PN: WingSpread Publishers, 1993.

Vincent, Marvin R. *Epistles to the Philippians and to Philemon*. ICC. Edinburgh: T. & T. Clark, 1968, 1979.

Wallace, Daniel B. *Greek Grammar: Beyond the Basics: An Exegetical Syntax of the New Testament*. Grand Rapids: Zondervan, 1996.

Welsey, Charles. "Jesus, Lover of My Soul." In *The Baptist Hymnal*, ed. Wesley L. Forbis, 180. Nashville: Convention Press, 1991.

————. "Jesus, Lover of My Soul." *Cyber Hymnal*. http://www.cyberhymnal.org/htm/j/l/jlmysoul.htm (accessed 1 July 2007).

Wilson, Amy. "Ahh, Learning Lessons, Again." Vologda, Russia: an unpublished email, 2008.

Witherington III, Ben. *The Paul Quest: The Renewed Quest for the Jew of Tarsus*. Downers Grove, IL: InterVarsity Press, 1998.

————. *Paul's Letter to the Romans: A Socio-Rhetorical Commentary*. Grand Rapids: William B. Eerdmans Publishing, 2004.